FIRING THE CLAY

FIRING THE CLAY

Occasional Writings of

ALAN ECCLESTONE

Edited by Jim Cotter

CAIRNS PUBLICATIONS · SHEFFIELD
in association with
ARTHUR JAMES
JOHN HUNT PUBLISHING · NEW ALRESFORD
1999

© Estate of Alan Ecclestone 1999

ISBN 0 85305 460 6

CAIRNS PUBLICATIONS
47 Firth Park Avenue, Sheffield S5 6HF

ARTHUR JAMES
an imprint of
JOHN HUNT PUBLISHERS
46a West Street, New Alresford
Hants SO24 9AU, United Kingdom

Further copies of this book
and other Cairns Publications
can be obtained from New Alresford.

Typeset in Monotype Baskerville by
Strathmore Publishing Services, London N7

Printed in Great Britain by
Biddles Ltd, Guildford and King's Lynn

CONTENTS

PREFACE

This is the fourth volume in an Alan Ecclestone Library. Cairns Publications has previously published his Book of Days, *Gather the Fragments*, a biography by Tim Gorringe, and 'thoughts for the day', quotations from the four books he wrote in his retirement, *Through the Year with Alan Ecclestone*.

He was much in demand as a lecturer, preacher, and retreat giver. Some of his addresses have appeared in print in a variety of magazines and books, some exist simply as handwritten manuscripts, undated and unpublished. This book offers a selection of these occasional pieces. Among them are his insights into what Karl Marx was really saying, clear of -ists and -isms. His concerns to connect prayer and political life, spirituality and the everyday, *mystique* and *politique*, are represented, not least by his small masterpiece, *On Praying*.

A short book, long out of print, on the Parish Meeting, his original contribution to parish strategy, is reproduced here: its feel is dated, but its content is as challenging as it ever was. Church polity was a minor concern, but he has trenchant things to say about disestablishment and about bishops, as well as an idiosyncratic piece on the custom at the Holy Communion of the Giving of the Peace – *On Living Oxymoronically*.

His second Bible was Shakespeare: he read all the plays once every year, and in his last months was intending to start learning the Sonnets by heart. So I am particularly pleased to have unearthed a somewhat sketchy and rough outline for what may have been two or three addresses. It is in his own hand, and I hope I have not misquoted either him or Shakespeare! His memory was phenomenal in extent, but not always absolutely accurate.

The selection finishes with pieces about a painting (Edvard

Munch's *The Scream*), a socialist (William Morris), a wedding, and a theological theme – transfiguration. The last points to the title of the book. Alan used to say that *Firing the Clay* would have been his choice of title for an autobiography: he was brought up in the Potteries, and in his own life showed something of that transformation of ordinary stuff of which the Transfiguration of Christ was both focus and model.

I should like to express my appreciation to those who sent me material for possible inclusion in this book. I am grateful to David Wilson who has given permission for his photograph of Alan Ecclestone to be reproduced, and I repair an omission here by acknowledging the same photograph in the book *Through the Year With Alan Ecclestone*. I also acknowledge permission from Martin Ecclestone to use the previously unpublished material, and from the various copyright holders of the pieces that have already appeared elsewhere.

JIM COTTER
Sheffield, August 1998

I

MARX: A MAN TO DISENTHRAL MANKIND

We obey the will of God when we leave the 'safe fortress' of our social shell and, on the horizon of the future allowed by God, we devote ourselves to the alteration of the world and thus enter into history itself.

J. MOLTMANN *Hope Without Faith*

I

Charles Kingsley's children are said to have asked him: 'Papa, who was Heine?' 'A bad man, my dears, a bad man.' It is a way of dealing with men and their purposes and ideas exceedingly popular still: you will hear it used every day of Marx, of Marxism and the Kremlin. It calls for both courage and patience, as well as knowledge, to resist this combination of ignorance, arrogance and stupidity, and that native brand of it which Dickens immortalized in Mr Podsnap's words, 'Not English'. That in itself makes speaking of Marx a difficult matter.

There is also something almost absurd in proposing to speak in a matter of minutes about a man's life-work, so packed with furious intensity of thought, and covering so immense a field of human activity, that something like fifty volumes are today required for its publication. The temptation to reduce it to already well-worn phrases, clichés and slogans is insidious; even the presentation of the *skeleton* of Marxist teaching can be a distorting of the picture one would wish to provide. There is also the difficulty to be faced that even in Marx's lifetime, and among those predisposed to welcome what he was saying, there were great differences of opinion about its meaning, and he would himself have insisted that it must be judged always in the light of ever-changing conditions, that it be regarded more as a *method of inquiry* than as a body of doctrine. May I quote to you the comment of Engels, made years after Marx had died? 'According to the materialist conception of history, the determining element in history is *ultimately* the production and reproduction in real life. *More than this neither Marx nor I have ever asserted.* If somebody twists this into the statement that the economic element is the *only* determining one, he transforms it into a meaningless, abstract and absurd phrase. The economic situation is the basis, but the various elements of the superstructure – political forms of the class struggle and its consequences, constitutions established by the victorious class after a successful battle etc. – forms of law – and then even the reflexes of all these actual struggles in the brains of the combatants: political, legal, philosophical themes, religious ideas and their further developments into systems of dogma, *also exercise their influence upon the course of historical struggles and in many cases preponderate in determining their form* ...' (From a letter to E. Bloch, 1890).

2

With that in mind, I must nevertheless risk an over-simplification in presenting Marx to you as a man who contributed much to the 'disenthralment of mankind'.

I have used this phrase for a number of reasons. Firstly, words and phrases like 'freedom', 'the free world', and 'being free', have now such spurious connotations that they resemble nothing so much as false currency.

Secondly, it was used by Abraham Lincoln at a critical time in American affairs to signify what he took to be his essential task, as well as that of the American people. 'Disenthralment' means *'being set free from bondage'* and for Jews and Christians it should mean a great deal: the Bible is a great book about it. Lincoln was reminding people that it did not just mean setting black slaves free from their hitherto white owners, but setting all men and

women, black and white, free from those notions about themselves, about other people, about the point and meaning of life,
which do darken minds and captivate human beings, making
them less humane, less loving, forgiving, just and merciful than
they might otherwise be.

Thirdly, I use it because Lincoln as well as Marx and a great
many others who have been concerned with disenthralment,
have inevitably been involved in *bitter conflict,* not of choice, but
because disenthralment itself is felt to be menacing to the power
and authority and well-being of those who control social life,
and provocative of disruption of what they assume to be the
God-given structure of society. Lincoln was no Marxist, but a
sensitive honest man put by history in just such a circumstance
as to compel him to act in ways which illustrate vividly all that
Marx was describing and analyzing in impersonal terms in his
life-work. The American Civil War, on which Marx's shrewd
comments are still worth reading, was but an incident in the
advance of Capitalist power, overthrowing an already archaic
economic/political order, not by any means for humanitarian
reasons, but because in the last resort an economic revolution
demanded it, and, in Engel's words, 'It is in the nature of all parties and classes which have come to power through revolution to
demand that the new basis of right created by the revolution
should also be unconditionally recognized and regarded as holy.'

My fourth reason is that this disenthralment must for ever be
regarded as 'open-ended'. Neither Marx nor any great teacher
has the whole truth; the best they can do is to help us to rid ourselves of the domination of our own creations, legal, political,
philosophical, religious. Marx was understandably reluctant to
picture the kind of society, whether called Fascist or Communist,
of the future, because he was well aware of the ever-present
temptation to manufacture new ideological structures and deem
them beyond dissent. Nicholas Lash has said, 'If Christian
discourse is not to become idolatrous, *it must be permanently
iconoclastic.'* This is a hard saying. Neither Christians nor
Marxists can be entirely comfortable with it, yet I believe that
both are committed to it, and that Marx, in spite of a frequently
dogmatic attitude, did try to honour it.

3

I have begun with the man who trod these Manchester streets in the hungry forties, and before going further, let me say that there was much about him that was unpleasant, much that remained implacably 'not English', much that bequeathed unhappiness and suffering to those who loved and revered him. In his work too, there was much that was frankly inadequate, even misleading, much that is the handicap of a great pioneer. He was at his vituperative worst – and he had very considerable talents here – in speaking of working-class leaders in Britain and elsewhere who annoyed him with their sectarian views. What he took to be the smug English habit of eschewing extremes reduced him to fury – not the best frame of mind to enable him to get them to understand what he was driving at.

But more important than this was the fact that when he came here in 1845 he had already gone far to work out the main lines of his subsequent work. These are set out later of course in the Communist Manifesto, but it is, I think, in the *German Ideology* – a somewhat tedious rag-bag of a book – that we find the sharp tools designed for our disenthralment. The first chapter, recently described by one scholar as 'the most central of Marx's texts', declared of his contemporaries that they 'have constantly made up for themselves false conceptions about themselves, about what they are, and what they ought to be. The phantoms of their brains have gained the mastery over them … let us liberate them from chimeras, the ideas, dogmas, imaginary beings under the yoke of which they are pining away.' If we ask how Marx proposed to effect that liberation, the answer must be by teaching them *the materialist conception of history*, and this by way of getting them to ask questions about that bit of history with which they themselves were immediately involved. It meant asking them to do more than protest against injustices or teach political doctrines or to organize parties, but to be as radical as possible in asking what were the forces at work which had brought into being and were now ceaselessly expanding the kind of society they now lived in – for which the word 'Capitalist' was beginning to be used. What were the actual relations of those working in it, what were the aims and consequences of it, what did it do to human beings? Wherein was it different from previous societies?

4

What was so particular about this? Human beings have discussed their political and social institutions for two millennia and more, and in modern Europe there were great leaders of oppressed people like Munzer and the Anabaptists, and others in the French Revolution. In England Winstanley and the Diggers, Lilburne and the Levellers, represented a vivid coming to consciousness of men and women concerned for a righteous and reasonable social order.

What was lacking from these movements was a critical analysis of the nature of society that could explain how it came about as well as how it actually functioned. To do justice to Marx we have to understand something at least of the extraordinary nature of the task he undertook. Put simply, we have to see him as the man who asked questions about the greatest industrial revolution in history. Because we are so used to that phrase 'industrial revolution' we may not believe that those who were deeply involved in it did not see it that way. 'No one had forecast the development of a machine-industry. Capitalism arrived unannounced,' (Polanyi) and the most far-reaching transformation of human society on a global basis had already begun by people who were almost entirely unconscious of its nature. They were quite unprepared to examine, much less to understand, the nature, the power, the thrust of the new technology and its bearing on human life.

Looking back we can see that they could not begin to do so until some pioneer could devise a method of inquiry, a hypothesis adequate to the task, an insight such as Darwin brought to natural history and Freud to human psychology. Marx believed that it was necessary to establish a sound empirical and scientific basis for any attempt to understand society's problems. What Darwin turned over in his mind while on board the *Beagle* and after, had its counterpart in Marx's reflections here in these

Manchester streets and in London as he set about studying the
phenomena of this revolutionary scene.

Let me add that in all such great leaps of understanding, later
ages may see faults and flaws, false and inadequate steps being
taken, but the overall scene has been changed for ever.
Humankind has moved into a new phase of self-understanding
through the work of such men. Sociology has developed, as
every great scientific discipline does, resisting, even rejecting,
what all great pioneers made use of, but its debt to them remains
and in field after field, Marx's influence may still be traced.

                                   5

Perhaps such an insight could have been gained only here in
England by a political exile with philosophical training and an
indebtedness to his Jewish forbears for a sense of history tipped
with apocalyptic expectations. Europe was still too obsessed with
the politics of the aftermath of the French Revolution to be
aware of the potentially more far-reaching revolution occurring
in Britain. Marx came here because the political struggles which
had made him already an avowed opponent of the régimes in
France, Germany and Belgium, left him no other alternative.
What the books in the Manchester Library on Economics to
which Engels introduced him (and later, those of the British
Museum) did, was to turn him into a revolutionary of a quite
different kind, one who revolutionized people's thinking about
human society, preparing the way for a world vision of human
affairs.

He came with already considerable resources for such a task:
a mind sharpened by Hegelian inquiry into the dynamics of history, and a capacity for grasping the empirical data required,
together with a passion for concentrating his great energy,
despite personal troubles, upon his self-chosen work. Where his
great genius lay was in his power to see certain features of this
fermenting human scene which made it explicable to the participants in it, to enable them to become no longer the blind
authors of its story but to an ever-increasing extent *the purposeful
makers of it.*

He had no illusions about the costliness of the task, either for himself or for those who would grasp the significance of his work, not simply because he knew what the lust for power and possessions does for human beings, but because he recognized something which we are still only beginning to explore of the way in which the human mind deals with our experience. The core of the Marxist understanding of the human condition lies not only in his perception that people produced themselves in the course of their productive labours, but that they also devised a way or ways of understanding this – something other than sense-perception – something which stretches all the way from ideologies to visions, and forms what has been called 'seeing with the eyes of the soul.' The problem faced by Marxism is the discrepancy between the world situation produced by people's productive activity and their understanding of it and of themselves engaged in it. Put very crudely, it contemplates human society in which advanced technologies are in the hands of those whose self-understanding is that of an archaic past.

I must not press this into the areas of depth-psychology, which are the fruits of twentieth century work, but emphasize only that Marx laid the foundations of such development in his analysis of the history of society, albeit in one very limited phase of it, that of the capitalist society developing round him.

6

Marx does not appear to have used the term 'historical materialism' to describe his basic contention, but it was by way of a materialist conception of history that he sought to explain how human beings have come to be what they are and to think as they do. He insisted that people shaped society and themselves through the relations they entered into in the economic sphere where they gained their bread. In this he helped to bring about a change in the writing of history itself. Remembering that Macaulay began to write his *History of England* in 1839, that a romantic amateur like Kingsley could in 1860 be appointed Regius Professor of Modern History at Cambridge (of whom one critic wrote: 'Other professors, whether competent or

incompetent, had at least *some* outward and visible connection
with the subjects they undertook to teach ... but of all men living
he is the least qualified to undertake the role of a historian'),
and, furthermore, that the planning of the Cambridge Modern
History Course as late as the turn of the century ignored almost
entirely any but the traditional political factors; we can appreciate today what the influence of Marx was to be! I do not want
to suggest that Marx alone made possible the writing of History
as we know it today, but that he contributed profoundly to it – as
is admitted by most historians today.

It is within this radically changed conception of history that
Marx formulated his teaching about the class struggle. He stated
it briefly in the Manifesto: 'The history of all human society,
past and present, has been the history of class-struggles,' and he
went on to add, 'Our own age, the bourgeois age, is distinguished by this – that it has simplified class and antagonisms.
More and more, society is splitting into two great hostile camps,
into two great and directly contraposed classes: bourgeois and
proletariat.'

Two comments on this are called for. Firstly, Marx never
claimed that he had discovered the existence of classes or the
class struggle in modern society, but that he had simply observed
what Ricardo and other economists had already shown. 'Long
before me,' he wrote, 'bourgeois historians had described the
historical development of this class-struggle and bourgeois
economists the economic autonomy of the classes. What I did
that was new was to prove, firstly, that the existence of classes is
only bound up with particular, historic phases in the development of production, secondly, that the class struggle necessarily
leads to the dictatorship of the proletariat, thirdly, that this
dictatorship itself only constitutes the transition to the abolition
of all classes and to a classless society.' Furthermore in a very
long letter addressed to Liebknecht and other leaders of the
German Social Democratic Party in Germany in 1879, Marx
and Engels repeated: 'For almost forty years we have stressed the
class-struggle as the immediate driving force of history, and in
particular the class-struggle between the bourgeoisie and the
proletariat as the great lever of the modern social revolution: it

is impossible for us to co-operate with people who wish to expunge this class-struggle from the movement.'

The second point that must then be made today concerns the relevance of this to the political scene a century later. It is a small but significant point that terms like 'proletariat' and 'bourgeoisie' have not become 'naturalized' in Britain, nor has the admitted 'class consciousness' which is noted by all students of British society developed the political militancy that would make it 'the great lever of social revolution'. The working class, writes Lichtheim, 'so far from generating a spontaneous drive towards socialist democracy, has shown an alarming tendency to acquiesce in patterns of sociopolitical domination which promise to guarantee economic advance and full employment at the cost of freedom.... The Marxian perspective of a socialist transformation propelled by labour's collective drive towards emancipation seems rather less plausible than it did a century ago.' What has happened in fact is the large-scale substitution of political/social reforms and economic gains for some sections of working people rather than an overall movement to bring into being a new socialist society, 'a totally novel culture, a new concept of reality and of human potentialities, new ways of incorporating the undivided biography into societal history and new patterns of inter-human relations rather than a mere institutional change in the titles of ownership or a reshuffling of the ruling garrison.'

7

Must we say that Marx was totally mistaken? That I think would be as great a misjudgement as that which fails to appreciate the extent of disintegration and loss of meaningful life in our modern sophisticated society. There can be no doubt that Marx did have great expectations. Changes in the economic foundations 'lead sooner or later to the transformation of the whole immense superstructure.' And it is likely that he did go through alternate phases of expecting a European revolution and reconciling himself to waiting longer. Similarly the emphasis he put upon alienation, though he used it less and less in his later writings, did remain basic to his teaching. 'The careful reader of *Capital*',

writes Baumann in *Socialism, The Active Utopia*, 'asks himself more
than once how Marx actually envisaged the chain of inevitabil-
ities which connects the appropriation of surplus value with a
socialist revolution. The answers varied, but none withstood a
close scrutiny. Was it the notorious contradiction between productive forces and productive relations? If so, who would be the
agent of change: managers, legislators? Would there be a total
collapse of the system, similar to that which occurred in slave
society? Or would there be a revolt born of destitution and
despair which might bring down the system of exploitation?
In the last case – does not the mitigation of poverty cancel the
prospect of socialism?'

8

It is not difficult to see from our vantage ground that prediction
at any time in the rapidly changing technological and political
world which Marx knew was a risky business, and he was usually
quick to notice new factors and quite ready to accept the need
for revising his work within the overall limits of his socialist
vision. What we can plainly see is that the unforeseen changes
were much more far-reaching than anyone could have dreamed.
Capitalism had, perhaps still has, a far greater resourcefulness as
well as technological possibilities, to secure to itself not only the
expanding labour power of the whole world, but to persuade a
substantial proportion of its vast army to accept its directives, to
divide and rule, to concede reforms, to exploit its control over
channels of communication. We are probably aware of the
likelihood of unforeseeable consequences of the several technological revolutions now proceeding, but we cannot do much
more than hazard some thought as to their nature. We know that
half a decade can now spring major developments upon us.

   On the other hand we cannot but be conscious that the world
situation does confront us with a scene of extreme bifurcation,
and that as the two Brandt Reports indicate, the gap between
the haves and have-nots is actually increasing. 'What capitalist
development has meant to the masses in countries like South
Korea, Taiwan, Singapore, Sri-Lanka, Pakistan, is increased

poverty. All the GNP they amass for their country through their incessant labour leaves them poorer than before. They produce what is of no real use to them, and yet they cannot buy what they produce – neither use-value nor exchange-value' (A. Sivanandan, *A Different Hunger*). We see that the forms of conflict change but we canot avoid confrontation with them.

It is worth noting that Marx frequently referred to Ireland, with comments like this: 'If the English army and police were withdrawn tomorrow (1870) you would at once have an agrarian revolution,' or again, 'I have come to the conclusion that the decisive blow against the English ruling classes (and it will be decisive for the workers' movement all over the world) cannot be delivered in England, but only in Ireland.' 'The special task of the Central Council in London is to awaken a consciousness in the English workers that for them the national emancipation of Ireland is no question of abstract justice or human sympathy but the first condition of their own emancipation.'

I would cite another reflection Marx made during the Franco-German War. 'What the Prussian fools do not see is that the present war is leading just as inevitably to a war between Germany and Russia, and a war of this kind will act as the midwife to the inevitable social revolution in Russia.'

What is much more important however than plotting out the lines of Marx's predictions is recognition on our part that he did leave his expressions of faith in the socialist outcome of the revolution lying ahead in such forms as 'led to a gross oversimplification of process ... a very serious underestimation of the difficulties of socialist institution-making ... a scepticism as to democratic values ... an undue optimism as to the revolutionary transformation of human nature.' But I fancy we could say much the same about Lincoln's speeches, and say of both men's faiths that they did not 'engender' these consequences 'but failed to anticipate them and warn against them'.

I would add that in respect of nationalism, art, literature, ethics and religion, it was the omissions from Marx's teaching that were to prove misleading. Marx, on the whole, kept himself in the 'rear of his affections', but his very determination to establish the historical objectivity of the movement of humankind towards a socialist society gave him opportunities to browbeat those who ventured to embody other judgements as to how this socialist revolution was to be brought about. There was nothing of the element of disclosure in his treatment of them. Again and again we are faced in the record by furious polemic against teachers and political leaders, most of whom are largely forgotten today, but with whom Marx believed he must settle accounts ...

Typical of it was his seething attack upon Weitling, a brilliant young tailor-agitator who in 1838 had become a popular leader of working class movements in Germany, France and Belgium. He met Marx in Brussels in 1846. In the midst of a public meeting in which he expounded his views, which Marx sarcastically described as 'communist propaganda which has won over so many workers that they had thereby lost their work and their bread,' Marx suddenly thundered: 'Tell us, Weitling, with what arguments do you defend your social revolutionary activity? And on what basis do you propose to ground them?' Weitling replied that his efforts for the common good in the name of Justice, Solidarity, and Brotherly Love which had brought him hundreds of grateful letters 'were more important than closet-analysis carried out far from the suffering world.' At that point Marx leapt to his feet, pounded the table and shouted: 'Ignorance has never helped anybody yet.' Thirty years later he was still fuming about Weitling.

Now we know that it is not enough to be well-meaning in the complicated situations of social life, that knowledge and expertise and theoretical understanding are essential for their right handling, and we know too that Marx was not oblivious to the fact that 'people, not things, and not the mighty course of events outside ourselves, write history.' He was too passionate a humanist to forget that, but his very absorption in the task he had outlined for himself did lead him to ignore or disparage other aspects of it in the fields I have mentioned.

He was profoundly concerned with the socialist movement in Britain; but British Socialism, as Tawney reminds us, had grown out of an impulse quite obstinately and unashamedly ethical in character. 'The revolt of ordinary men against Capitalism', he wrote, 'has its source, neither in the obvious deficiencies as an economic engine, nor in the conviction that it represents a stage in social evolution now outgrown, but in the straightforward hatred of a system that stunts personality and corrupts human relations by permitting the use of men by man as an instrument of pecuniary gain.' Marx believed that this kind of approach too easily substituted idealist notions where only a hard scientific foundation could support revolutionary action. He commented sourly on the British parliamentary elections of 1868 'Once again the proletariat has discredited itself terribly ... everywhere the rag tag and bobtail of the official parties – a hopeless certificate of destitution.... The parson has shown unexpected power and so has the cringing to respectability.'

9

Now it is not just his concentration on 'economic man' that led Marx to narrow the field as he did. He came to his life's work as a philosopher concerned to attack philosophical idealism in all its forms. In his *Critique of Hegel's Philosophy of Right* he had published those words by which almost alone he is known to millions of non-readers today: 'Religion is the sigh of the oppressed creature, the sentiment of the heartless worlds, the soul of soul-less conditions, the opium of the people.' He had, when he came to England, settled his accounts with theologians (a formidable task in contemporary Germany), declaring that the criticisms of religion, the premise of all criticism, had been completed. He had noted what Feuerbach had had to say of the essence of Christianity, and had stepped over and beyond that fiery brook to insist that the criticism be now carried further to those economic and social conditions which gave scope and nurture to idealistic religion.

That battle for disenthralment is still on, revealing much of the truth of Marx's indictment of it, and even more of his inadequate understanding of the Christian religion. Since there is no time to develop this, I must simply refer you to such present day Marxist works as Ernest Bloch's *Man on His Own* and Goldmann's *The Hidden God*, but to quote from John MacMurray who taught philosophy here in Manchester briefly, years ago,

whose *Search for Reality in Religion* says: 'I was wholly convinced by
Marx that idealism is a dangerous illusion which must be rejected – idealist religion is unreal, but I was not convinced that
religion is necessarily a form of idealism.' And so he felt himself
committed to the rediscovery of a Christianity which was non-
idealist. 'A spirituality that does not seek and secure its material
embodiment is imaginary and unreal. A material life that is not
spiritually directed is a meaningless quest for power and more
power for its own sake.'

I suggest that much Christian thinking has moved towards
dialogue with Marxism for this very reason, and the debt to him
should be acknowledged. Basic questions he raised have still to
be faced. How had human society – the society of Christendom
– and so called Christian civilized society come to be what it
was? Why did so many people acquiesce in such a humanly
degrading, impoverished social life? Why did so many efforts to
mitigate the cruelty of the conditions in which men, women and
children were condemned to live, meet with such implacable
opposition? How could intelligent and supposedly sensitive
people acquiesce in the comment made upon Mayhew's revelations of working-class life in London! 'There is no one to blame
for this: it is the result of Nature's simplest laws.' Perhaps they
really believed it – and Marx did not blame them for this; he
simply sought to inquire why they did so. He recognized that
'few men believed that society was a man-made thing, serving in
the first place the interests of those who controlled it: it was to
them divinely ordained. So those who controlled it believed that
it not only worked that way, but must be allowed without interference to do so.' Where Capitalist society differed from its pre-
decessors was in its attempt to combine divine approach for 'the
powers that be' with an economic literalism which devised its
own symbols either as convenient slogans or under the illusion
they were descriptions, '*laissez faire*' being one of its prime examples, the 'survival of the fittest' another.

It is not difficult to document this. It is possibly a measure of
Marx's success that we may find it hard to believe that human
beings could have produced such nauseating stuff. In 1795, e.g.
in his *Thoughts and Details on Scarcity* (i.e. on some people dying of

starvation), Burke wrote: 'One ought manfully to resist the very first idea, speculative or practised, that it is within the competence of Government, or even of the rich, as rich, to supply the poor with the necessaries which it has pleased the Divine Providence for a while to withhold from them. We, the people, ought to be made more sensible that it is not in breaking the laws of Commerce, which are the laws of Nature, and consequently the Laws of God, that we are to place our hope of softening the Divine displeasure to remove any calamity which we suffer or which hangs over us.' God had provided for the poor a suitable consolation in the hope of a better life in another world, and therefore 'Whoever deprives them of this consolation deadens their industry and strikes at the root of all acquisition as of all conservation.'

Whether this doctrine was as consoling to the poor as it was gratifying to the rich is open to question, but not so in minds like that of the distinguished Archdeacon Paley. In his infamous *Reasons for Contentment addressed to the Labouring Part of the British Public* in 1793, he remarked that 'Religion smooths all inequalities because it unfolds a prospect which makes all earthly distinctions nothing.' It was strange to notice how the possessors of inequalities on one side of the ledger so desperately defended their 'nothings'. Marx simply observed this and commented: 'The ideas of the ruling class are in every epoch the ruling ideas, and these are nothing more than the ideal expression of the dominant material relations – the dominant materials grasped as ideas.'

Does this mean that disenthralment in the sphere of religion is an as yet unfinished work – indeed, a task never to be completed since humankind so perversely threatens to renew its old fetishes, not least in times of stress which are likely in our age to be many? I think that it does. It is nonetheless a complex affair. We can of course see its manifestation in 'liberation theology' as put forward most strikingly by Latin Americans like Bonino, Guttierez, Assman, Segundo, and by both Asians and Africans in slightly changed terms, though the connection with economic and political liberation of the vast proletariat for which they speak is everywhere evident. As Bonino expounds it, it means simply that 'we cannot receive theological interpretation coming

from the rich world without suspecting it and asking what kind
of practice it supports, reflects and legitimizes.' Christianity
must be verified in relation to such matters as imperialism, political and economic, apartheid, self-determination and personal
equality.

It simply will not do for the representatives of the rich powerful world to deplore those whom they call 'political priests' as if
they were simply undercover agents of Moscow. The extent of
revolutionary significance cannot be avoided: the co-existence of
these great masses of poor and rich people cannot go on much
longer. The disenthralment of minds of which Marx is both
agent and symbol has passed a point of no return. I quote a
leading black novelist, Chinua Achebe: 'In confronting the black
man, the white man has a simple choice: either to accept the
black man's humanity and equality or to reject them and see him
as a beast of burden. No middle course exists as an intellectual
quibble. For centuries Europe has chosen the beastly alternative
...' Or as James Cone put it: 'Liberation is not only consistent
with the gospel – it is the gospel. There can be no theology
which is not identified unreservedly with those who are humili-
ated and abused.' These are the echoes a century later of Marx's
words: 'The worker has become a commodity, and he is fortunate if he can find a buyer. His place in society is determined by
those able to buy him: thus the capitalist-social economy pro-
pounds the thesis that the worker, like a horse, must receive just
as much as will enable him to work.'

A caveat: We must needs recognize what a spokesman for the
black community has written: 'If the white worker's lot at the
hands of capitalism was alienation, the blacks underwent complete deracination. And it is this factor which makes black
oppression qualitatively different from the oppression of the
white class.... White Marxists (Marxism, after all, was formulated in a European context and must be, on its own showing,
Eurocentric) have ignored the importance of its existential
consequences – in effect its consequences to culture. The whole
structure of white racism is built no doubt on economic exploitation, but it is cemented with white culture.'

Something of the same must be said today also in regard to

the exploitation of human beings sexually – the oppression of women. It was not that Marx did not see this, but he did not feel or appreciate its true significance.

And the religious question is as alive as ever, not for the security of established churches, but for the grappling with the transcendent aspects of human life which capitalism ignores.

10

What I want chiefly to leave with you then, is that the preliminary critique that Marx declared to have been completed – i.e. in the sphere of religion – is, in the very material terms to which a Marxist must refer for its verification, by no means completed. But in its non-idealist characterization of religion it is the storm centre of the approaching world revolution. The irony of this must be acknowledged, but it is, if we look closely at it, no more than a projection onto the world's screen of the Bible's typology. We have but found other words and gestures with which to clothe it. Marx himself in the early writings now known as the *Economic and Philosophical Manuscripts* took up the Hegelian concept of alienation and turned it round, making it a key concept of his entire work. 'The propertied class and the class of the proletariat represent the same human self-alienation.' The word has become today almost overworked in attempts to describe our human condition. 'Never before', Herbert Read wrote in his *Art and Alienation* (1967) 'in the history of our Western world has the divorce between man and nature, between man and his fellow man, between individual man and his selfhood been so complete. Such is one of the main effects of that system of production we call capitalism as Marx foresaw.' He went on to add: 'The possibility of alienation exists wherever social and political developments denote feelings of anxiety and despair, of rootlessness and insecurity, of isolation and apathy.' Read's words need to be sharpened. Alienation is not just divorce – it is the subjection of relations between human beings to a form of relations between things, the *subordination* of all human relations – loving – enjoying – forgiving – to that of the market. There must be no interference with market conditions, no measure of policy countenanced that would influence the action of these markets. To include all elements, labour, land, money, people, in the market mechanism means to subordinate the substance of society itself to the laws of the market.

In such a condition, Marx insisted, human beings, the makers of the historical process, growing, loving, relating, have been alienated, sold and bound to the inhuman power of Capital. He then made a great gesture of faith: that the inevitable self-destruction of so inhuman a system, whether in terms of nihilism, warfare, exhaustion, madness of its subjects, would in fact be carried out by the workers brought into class-consciousness by the system to seek an alternative human society.

Marx was not alone in this thought of approaching convulsion. 'What Nietzsche's thought proclaims', it has been said, 'is not so much the death of God as the death of his murderer, man.' Secularization has not proved to be more liberating than its religious alternatives, though Marx remained hopeful of the ultimate liberation of the oppressed.

His gesture of faith may have been misplaced, but what we owe to him in this matter of disenthralment is substantially what we owe to all great prophets who open our eyes to the fetishes, images, illusions, fantasies which we construct for our own enslavement. The tragic aspect of human history lies not simply in the fact that we build the tombs of the prophets whom we kill or deny or reject, but that we build our own prison-houses and fawn upon our own self-created gaolers. Marx laid bare to our eyes how our up-to-date version of the most ancient beguilement of humankind was built and fastened upon human lives. That in itself was a marvellous achievement – hence the words I have used of him – but it is not enough. It is not my business here to examine what others like Lenin, Luxembourg, Gramsci, and Mao Tse Tung, tried to do to effect the process of liberation, but simply to add what I as a Christian, deeply indebted to Marx, would wish to add. It is the critique and the discipleship which I see embodied in Jesus Christ which offers a greater hope. I put it no further than that, 'a discipleship willing to create and keep open the possibilities for reconciliation, redemption and community.' It is in that that the process of disenthralment consists.

2

WITH MARX FOR CHRIST

Once, people asked, 'What has Christ to do with Apollo?' Today they may well ask, 'What has Christ to do with Marx?' Indeed, they are being compelled to do so, not because some Marxists pursue anti-God campaigns, or because Marx made a few much-quoted but largely misapplied remarks about religion, or even because larger areas of the world are governed by people professing to be Marxist in outlook, but because Marx has changed the thinking of humankind to a very considerable extent, and, in doing so, altered the 'world' with which Christians have to do.

Either way, whether abhorred as the great enemy of the faith or welcomed as one who has opened our eyes, Marx has to be reckoned with as a force in human life. The shift from a pagan deity to a human teacher in our question is itself a sign of the times, a sign of changed thinking about the Christian faith, an indication of the direction in which further change is likely to be made. The question is not to be evaded because Christ had some hard things to say about those who failed to notice and read aright the signs of the times.

As a Christian I want to begin with Christ. What does it mean to be 'for Christ'? I believe that by it Christians are committed to an active concern for the salvation of the world, i.e. for the health or right living of the whole body of humankind, for right relationships between persons, men and women alike, who make up that body, for right dealing with each person, greatest or least, within it, for the pursuit of such truth and understanding as are needed to see in what this rightness consists and how it may be established, in what ways and for what reasons it is anywhere being rejected or thwarted in our ways of living, and how it may be recovered and nurtured to greater strength. To worship God

19

'through Christ' is to be involved in this multiform concern for
the Body whose Head is Christ, a Body as yet being put to shame
but one day to be wholly glorified.

I put it this way because Christians were warned a long time
ago not to delude themselves into coming before God with their
relations with other people unexamined. Long before Christ
indeed, the true service of God had been described by one of his
own people as the taking off of the yoke from the oppressed and
the feeding of the hungry, not as the whole of that service, no
doubt, but as an essential pre-requisite. The test still stands. It is
still as awkward a matter as ever, for Christians are not permitted any more than Marxists to divide theory from practice, and
in parts of the world where Christians have had for many centuries a near-monopoly of authority 'the hungry sheep look up
and are not fed.' In the light of its own title-deeds the record of
the Christian Church is a bad one. It has too often been more
pre-occupied with authority than with service, with dogma more
than with inquiry, with conformity more than with freedom.
Persecution, a sign of deep inner faithlessness, has stained a
great part of this history with abominable cruelty. At the time of
the St Bartholomew Day Massacre the papal nuncio reported to
Rome that only the King of France 'had acted in the spirit of a
Christian and refrained from mercy.' How could such things be?

Marx is to be seen and welcomed first of all as one who has
helped us to look a bit more closely at history, to understand a bit
better not only how men and women's lives, the stuff of history,
are shaped but also how the writing of history has been wittingly
and unwittingly slanted. To be rid of such treasonable practices
we need to be helped to see how the fears and assumptions per-
taining to the social conditions in which people live do limit their
vision. Marx traced a good deal of this distorted vision to the
influence of the basic conditions that governed their lives, to the
ways in which they gained their bread or cake, to the social relations in which they were involved in getting them.

He did not say, as some people seem to imagine, that these
economic factors were wholly determinative of people's lives,
but he did insist that their influence was more subtle and per-
vasive than had so far been seen, and that their operation in

changing the course of history was more powerful than historians had yet admitted. Difficult as it must always be to become aware of the blind spots in one's vision, to distinguish the ideological slant that bends all our perceptions, he nevertheless proposed to make the effort to do so. So too did Christ. The rich, as a parable made clear, could quite fail to notice the poor at their gates and would not even take notice though one rose from the dead to remind them. How blind could you get and why? Marxism is really a prolonged effort to try to see some of these unnoticed things.

Let me say at once that neither Marx nor his followers have managed to free themselves from ideological distortions. Marxists have done their worst in turning Marx into a dogmatic authority. Marx himself was too much a child of the age in which it was believed that a scientific explanation of all human affairs could be found and utilized as a key to their satisfactory resolution to be as wise as the situation demanded. Today we are more likely to see that the arts can give us as much, if not more, insight into human affairs (or that scientific concepts have taken on a new character) than the rather mechanical idea of scientific forces that obtained when Marx was writing. But this does not mean that we can ignore those things which he did see with a new clarity.

Marxism begins, as all good teaching does, with asking questions or, as Pieter Geyl would say of history, by making criticisms. The starting-place for an understanding of it (whether you regard it as friend or foe) is not the Socialist Society or the present state of the USSR or China, not dialectical materialism or democratic centralism or the Communist Manifesto, but a questioning, a never-to-be-concluded questioning about the nature of human history. It questioned the adequacy of the history then being accepted and it should today, if rightly used, compel us to go on questioning. It is a radical process of questioning quite explicit about the root matter it seeks to elucidate. It asks 'What does it mean to be human?' For this it has good biblical authority, and in its own way it is repeating the scandalous question 'Who do men say that I, the son of man, am?' It still produces the disturbances it once did. Marx saw that most people don't want to face this question because they have already to their own satisfaction answered it, because they are living in a world that has, as part of its answer, divided humankind (he called it 'species-man') into strange grades-men, not-quite-men, and men who look like men but are not men at all; a world that could only think of women in terms of their relationship to men!

Marx pressed home his question. Why was it that people were unwilling to answer? How did it come about that one person could see another not as a human being at all but as vermin? 'Nobody was hurt, only two or three niggers got killed.' 'To be able to see Nobody, and at that distance too', was not quite such a feat as the White King imagined; it is done everyday in the world we live in. Only radical questioning compels us to ask 'When is a human being somebody or nobody, a hand, unwanted labour, or an alien?' To ask the question at all we have to learn to stand outside the ideological assumptions of society that go so far to determine how human beings see at all. *Howards End* is a good novel to study for that purpose.

Now this prolonged effort to see human beings, rather than niggers, Jews, heretics, reds (the list is infinite) makes use of certain clues. The first is to be found in work, in what people are making and in what happens to what they make. Marx is like a geologist who asks 'What has this pebble got to teach me?' He asks 'What has this cotton-thread, this billet of steel, this standardized screw, this note of credit, got to teach me?' He does not stop questioning even when each and all of them have disclosed the complex ramifications of an industrial and commercial society, the divisions of labour, the skills bought and sold, the mechanized processes, the credits bespoken, because he must find out how and why they are all in process of change. It occurs to him that this vast productive enterprise, this outcome of human labour, has assumed an independent power that dominates and controls human lives. He sees humankind estranged from its own handiwork. He sees men and women estranged because of it from each other, from their own human nature, from the earth itself, by the enforced requirements of this Leviathan. He sees some people compelled to stand idle or to starve because Leviathan does not need them, sees others forced into life-destroying toil and ruthlessly driven to meet Leviathan's demands, sees others planning to encompass sea and land to make it yield more for Leviathan's enrichment. It is a picture so terrible that Moloch and Juggernaut seem crude by comparison.

But Marx does not stop questioning. To be human is to believe in human dignity, in reason, in beauty, in goodness. To be a humanist as Marx is is to believe that these things can prevail, to hold on to that belief even when you have nothing else left but hope. In the meanwhile he asks 'How?' He scans this same picture for clues to redemption. He insists that it is not by indulging in fantasy but by knowing and acting in this terrible world of reality that the way to redemption is to be found. He admits that religion has helped men and women to go on living in Hell's despite, but such religion is not enough. He must find a clue to an emancipation of humankind, and find it at work in the world.

Iris Murdoch has said that it is important to notice what human beings are afraid of. Apply that insight as Marx did to nineteenth-century England and you could see an answer, for example, in the Combination Laws. The very word 'combination' spelt something fearful to the established order. In it you would find the clue that Marx was looking for: the growth of a class-consciousness among those who must sell themselves in order to exist. Class-consciousness growing into and by means of class-conflict would school people to understand their condition, to understand themselves, to begin the re-creation of society. Tempered by the fires of such conflict they would 'learn by going where they have to go.' Leviathan himself would discipline them the world over. What they needed was a self-consciousness that would direct their going in the Exodus they must make. It was the problem that Moses and Mao-Tse-Tung had faced. It was the spirit that had summoned John Ball, Thomas Munzer, Gerard Winstanley, Joe Hill to act.

> From San Diego up to Maine,
> In every mine and mill,
> Where working men defend their rights
> Says he, 'You'll find Joe Hill.'

Marxism is concerned both with finding Joe Hill and helping him to find himself. Contrary to popular misjudgement it knows no easy answer to that problem because Leviathan in its form of Monopoly-Capitalism among its huge resources has great skills in supplying deceptive images for 'the likes of us'. It has not been difficult to set white against black, Aryan against Jew, Catholic against Protestant, tribe against tribe, or to portray class-conflict as a wicked device of subversive people to disrupt the good order of society. In the last resort, when all else fails, 'I can hire one half of the working class to shoot down the other half.' It is a very Long March that lies ahead but Marx never doubted that men driven to undertake it would learn to carry it to successful conclusion.

The last word must be questioned too. Marx was not sold to any conclusions about the future of human society, not even to communism as a final form. His great exemplar was Abraham going out into an unknown future and he had his dreams, but it was the immediate going that concerned him. It was not his business to foment revolutions or to stir up strikes but to help men and women to learn from their going, to unite them in the harsh process of their education, to summon them to fight back and to discover their humanity in so doing. He met the difficulties in his own flesh. He could be angry, embittered, scheming, spiteful like any other man. But he also knew that the thing he was after was much bigger than that, that the conflict was not so much against flesh and blood, capitalists, bourgeois, racists and the like, but against falsehood that took their flesh and used their resources of mind and wealth to pervert human life. Right relationships could only come into the world when men and women became aware of what they did to themselves and others, what they left undone, and what they failed to see as the truth of their own actions. I have described such work as eye-opening, a necessary step to the grasp of the truth of our human condition without which men and women cannot be at one with each other or themselves or, as Christians would say, with God. I see his work as a remedy for a great neglect on the part of Christians who have acquiesced for too long in blindness and with closed eyes. I see him as a servant of God, for God is certainly found by those 'who sought him not', and our patterns of servanthood have in any case been woefully defective. Christians are familiar with the imagery of the trumpet sounding: it would be well if they learned from Marx to hear its notes in 'Arise, ye starvelings, from your slumbers, Arise, ye criminals of want.'

3

MYSTIQUE AND POLITIQUE

There is no end to the praises that can be sung
of politics. In politics, not in economics, is found
the creative dialectic of opposites: for politics is
a bold prudence, a diverse unity, an armed
conciliation, a natural artifice, a creative compromise, and a serious game on which free civilization depends; it is a reforming conserver, a
sceptical believer, and a pluralistic moralist; it
has a lively sobriety, a complex simplicity, an
untidy elegance, a rough civility, and an ever-
lasting immediacy; it is a conflict become discussion; and it sets us a humane task on a
humane scale.

BERNARD CRICK *In Defence of Politics*

Do we really need to say more? Is it just foolishness to murmur
something about spirituality? It may be suspected that the
majority of the English would resent questions that implied that
they had not thought deeply and adequately about their politics
or that they might have much to learn from aliens about the
bearing of religion upon the matter. Dickens, as usual, hit the
nail on the head firmly. '"Never with my consent – not English,"
cried Mr Podsnap, to be greeted with an approving murmur
from the heads of the tribes.' Matthew Arnold, we know, raised
a critical voice but neither the Philistines nor the Barbarians
were seriously disturbed – 'Things are as they are.' There was
something almost sublime about such banality.

Perhaps we can no longer afford it. A book like Charles
Elliott's *Inflation and the Compromised Church* has made the point

and demanded 'radical contemplation as the only adequate basis for the radical restructuring of the Church which the facts of the situation demand.' But what does such a phrase mean? Embedded in English history there are numerous examples of radical demands, and a close study, for example, of the great Civil War, brings many of them to light. But radicalism itself can become a very tarnished coin. Was not Joseph Chamberlain deemed a 'radical'? The truth is that as a nation we are not disposed to welcome such demands. We do not take kindly to being asked to choose between the *Zéro de cité* and the city of God, between *la politique d'abord* and the presence of God in the world. One has to choose foreign terms to spell out what is at stake and translate them as best one can. 'The revolution will be moral or there will not be any,' wrote Charles Péguy, but what is this revolution that he speaks of? It is not easily translatable into the vocabulary of English political life.

There is no reason to suppose that the last quarter of the twentieth century will be less charged with national and international disputes, crises, conflicts, and catastrophes than the preceding years. Those who are summoned to prayer in our churches and those who endeavour to pray elsewhere may quite rightly ask to be helped to set about doing it with more clarified purpose. It is not difficult to come before the Lord with our present concerns (even for rivers of oil) made up and presented for blessing. It is much more difficult to see that the truth of Christian prayer demands a stripping-down, a purgation, an emptying out of interests that we call our own, to make room for interests that are God's. In faith we may believe that his take care of ours, but it is never easy to get that perspective right. Radical contemplation is concerned with a deepening awareness of how people and nations stand with God.

Our past history gives us little help. It is not simply that we have no experience in modern times comparable to the *Kulturkampf* or to the warfare of such men as Jules Combes and Charles Maurras – perhaps we are the better for that – but that neither our political nor our spiritual wrestlings have ever touched the great issues in terms like those employed by the Hebrew prophets. The so-called radical movements within and

without the churches not only failed to influence to any depth
the politics of the time, but more disastrously, failed to nurture a
spirituality alert to and discerning of the significance of the
social, economic, and political changes going on. Had the
Church of England been faced with the harsh travail that came
upon the Confessing Church in Germany, it is doubtful whether
it would have been any the better for preparing to bear witness
to the rejected Man of Sorrows. A 'genius for improvisation' is
no substitute for either radical questioning or radical
affirmation. Christians in England have not been accustomed to
the thought that their culture, which had once been Christian,
might not continue to be so any longer; not been prepared to see
that this involved them in a personal problem of choice; not
been troubled above measure by the anguish of either/or.
Kierkegaard who had said these things was not their prophet.

It has been said with truth that Revolution means 'a search
into the inexhaustible resources of the interior life,' means being
prepared to be troubled in spirit till the heart is broken, being
ready to come broken in heart to the place where the temporal
and the eternal meet. Otherwise we are more likely to invoke the
God of Battles to fight our own and to subscribe to the bitter
joke of *Catch 22*, of being confounded to learn that God listens
to the prayers of lesser breeds than our own. It means recogniz-
ing that while a profound simplicity may attend the end-product
of prayer, it is not reached by any by-passing of the difficulties.

Among those who can best help us to set about the task,
Charles Péguy still waits to be heard. 'Everything depends upon
the dovetailing of the temporal and the eternal. Everything col-
lapses once that adjustment is unsettled or out of true or taken
to pieces.' Here too speaks the resolute opponent of political
ecclesiastics and their henchmen. 'Because they have no temporal courage they think they have penetrated to the eternal.
Because they love no one, they think they love God.' We are
dealing with a poet, a political warrior, a pamphleteer of genius,
but above all with a man of prayer who, as he said, 'had fought
all his life upon the frontiers,' and despite his passionate love for
friends, family, and France ventured everything in his quest for
the truth in God. Alain-Fournier's much quoted words deserve

repeating: 'I say, knowing what I am saying, that not since Dostoevsky has there been a man who was so clearly a man of God.'

Péguy was involved in politics from his earliest years, in the tortuous and bitter politics of the Third Republic. At fourteen he wrote of Socialism as 'a new life, not just a policy', at twenty-six he attacked Jules Guesde for being, despite all his authority as a Marxist, ignorant of Socialism. At thirty he was accusing Jaurés of prostituting his great powers for the sake of political expediency. A few years later he broke with Georges Sorel. For workmen on strike he was always ready to beg; for peasants and craftsmen he was intimately and perceptively concerned. Like his widowed mother he was ready to work sixteen hours a day. In 1899 he offered himself to the *Parti Ouvrier Français* of Orléans as a candidate for the First General Congress of the Socialist Party. By that time he was a seasoned fighter in the Dreyfusard battles.

Péguy's contribution to the right relating of politics and prayer was made both in his poetry and in the *Cahiers de la Quinzaine* which he published between 1900 and his death in 1914. A large proportion of this work was devoted to the discussion of political problems in almost every country of the world as well as to the immediate issues of French politics during the bitter years of the *Affaire* and the Church-State conflict which split open French society. These are the years in which schoolchildren could be paraded in the streets to howl 'Death to the Jews', in which a cabinet minister could exult in putting out the lights of heaven, in which army officers spied upon and denounced each other for their religious affiliations. Almost all the repulsive features of anti-semitism, demagogy, financial trickery, and political thuggery which were later to assume such monstrous proportions in European life were evident already in the politics of France. Today a film by Jean Chérasse entitled *Dreyfus ou l'intolérable vérité* makes clear that the battle is still on. (A granddaughter of Dreyfus died at Auschwitz.) It was in that situation that Péguy contended for 'humanity at the price of God'.

It must be remembered too that during these years Péguy was fighting his own spiritual warfare, finding his way to faith and

exulting in grace yet obstinately remaining outside the communion of the Church. His situation to most people looked absurd:
a father who did not have his children baptized but who handed
them over in his anguished prayers to the Blessed Virgin when
they were sick and plodded out a pilgrimage to Chartres to do it,
a Catholic who didn't go to Mass, a Socialist who attacked class
warfare as a bourgeois conception, a party member who repudi-
ated the authoritarian structure of the party, what a grotesque
creature the man was! The fierce denunciations he made of
others, even of his closest friends when they appeared to him to
be traitors to the cause of truth and freedom, snapped the ties
with almost all he loved. This desperately lonely, hungry, and
overworked man yielded nothing in his devotion to the Hidden
God and the Incarnate Lord and the Virgin Mother.

The heart of Péguy's contribution to the matter of spirituality and politics lay in the *Cahier* which he wrote in 1910 entitled
Notre Jeunesse. Romain Rolland called it *'un cahier d'exultation mystique'*. It was written as a reply to Halévy's paper on the Dreyfus
affair seen in retrospect, which Péguy had published a few
months before. It was in character that it should be a fierce
riposte directed against one of his closest friends. Péguy insists
that the *Affaire*, which so many people on both sides were already
disposed to forget or ignore, had all the importance of a revelation, a moment of truth, which must not be lost to sight. The
cause could be betrayed all over again by those too careless to
stay awake, too willing to suppress the truth for the sake of
accommodation with new friends or for the appearance of
unanimity, too anxious to be successful and efficient in *le monde
moderne*.

It was in this *Cahier* that Péguy wrote most deliberately of the
distinction to be drawn between *mystique* and *politique* . He was to
return to it often, as indeed he did with all the major themes of
his life's work. Péguy's statement that everything begins in *mystique* and ends in *politique* has been quoted so often that its real
implications have largely been lost to sight. It is mishandled and
misused the moment it gets divorced from prayer. Its importance
lies in setting prayer to its task. Few men and women living,
working, and contending in the world of politics have ever

believed so passionately, ever lived their lives so deliberately on the basis of the moment-to-moment necessity of prayer or come to the discussion of political questions so directly from the position of a suppliant waiting upon God. 'Mysticism may be the laughing-stock of politics, but all the same it is the mystic who nourishes politics. They say they are practical and that we are not. That is precisely where they are mistaken.'

What then did Péguy mean by *mystique* and *politique*?

In his translation of Péguy's work on this theme, published under the title *Temporal and Eternal* (1958), Alexander Dru observed that the first version of the essay '*Clio*' described the source of *mystique* in terms of Christ's ministry on earth. *Mystique* had to be earthed in the social and political life of human beings. The *mystique* of any regime (and Péguy saluted the monarchy of St Louis no less fervently than the Republic of '93 and hailed the coming of Socialist society with equal warmth) lay in its embodiment of some essential features of the holy community which Christ has sown and nurtured in the soil of the earth. No form was perfect and final, nor was there anything to be said for endeavouring to cultivate the *mystique* of a long-vanished regime. Péguy was recklessly generous in his perception of the various expressions of *mystique*, and quite ready to say that the quarrel between them was of an utterly different character from their struggle with *politique*. Men and women needed to learn from the *mystiques* of the past how to address themselves to the task today. In his own view of them he wrote, 'The Republican *mystique* was when one died for the Republic; the republican *politique* is, as at the present, that one should live off it.'

It was this parasitic aspect of a *politique* which attacked both religious and political bodies that revolted him. Indeed, he saw it as most insidiously at work in the Church itself under the cover of a false *mystique*. 'The political forces of the Church have always been against its *mystique*,' and the success of such *politique* was evident in a growing sterility, an arid secularization, a mortification of the life of the body. 'Even our miseries are no longer Christian.'

The choice to be made in any political decision had to be seen as involving 'the opportunity for the regeneration of the

whole people'; it had to be weighed as helpful or hostile to the
spiritual health of the nation. Christians were not being required to come up with successful programmes but to be faithful in their witness to God in whatever was being decided. Péguy
saw his own work to lie precisely in the effort to lay bare before
the eyes of humanity the kind of opportunity and responsibility
laid upon them. The Old Testament demand, 'Choose life,' was
an immediate reality. Choices in the world of politics involved
the redemption or the enslavement of a whole people. The burden of his great poem upon Joan of Arc is not simply the liberation of France from the invader in terms of military success,
but the liberation of the souls of a people from cynical despair
and spiritual death. We read it today in a yet wider context, not
now of medieval France, but of the Republic, of the Resistance,
of the Third World peoples struggling to withstand the corruption of *politique*. We have grown accustomed to hearing all
political questions discussed in terms of economic or military
advantage. Péguy was insistent that they must be seen in terms
of moral obligation. 'A social body', he wrote, 'is in a state of
oppression when one single one of its members is oppressed.' It
was the business of *mystique* to search out such oppression and
cry aloud for relief. Pascal had summoned humanity to stay
awake in the presence of Christ's agony in the world; it was
Péguy's work to particularize the blows and the mockeries that
made it a continuing reality.

An obvious example lay in the *Affaire. Mystique* demanded the
exercise of a double courage. It was necessary in the first place
to proclaim the innocence of Alfred Dreyfus and to put everything in the life of the State, including its army and judicial
system, at question, to wager the total peace of society for this
one man's sake. *Mystique* could perceive that on the fate of this
single Jew the spiritual life of modern France was at stake. It was
necessary too that the matter should become personal, that one
should admit to oneself that Dreyfus was innocent and for that
reason sacrifice peace of mind and heart in the struggle to be
waged on his behalf. 'They, our adversaries, aimed at temporal
salvation; we are determined that France should not fall into a
state of mortal sin.'

It was this concern for sin and salvation, for the spiritual
health or death of the nation, that made Péguy's treatment of
politics sound strange then, and still does so today. A social con-
tract is more recognizable, more easily manipulated, than a
covenant with God. It seems more likely to be workable.
'Hawking round one's conscience' does not commend itself to
severely practical people. Parties and programmes have been
devised for more limited objectives. We are likely to hear that
conscience is a thing that in time of crisis we cannot afford and
that many consciences are too narrowly framed.

Yet as we hear it said, as we reflect upon Péguy's description
of the descent from *mystique* to *politique*, we might well ask
whether we can afford not to be awake to the agony of the Son
of Man in our midst. To give the impression that all that happened a long time ago and that it is a closed chapter in human
history, if indeed it be history at all, is to sacrifice the *mystique*
implicit in our present-day problems. Remembering that tragi-
comical comment in *The Tempest* when men cry 'All lost, to
prayers, to prayers,' we may appreciate the intensity with which
Péguy, like Kierkegaard before him, rejected this reduction of
God to the status of a last-resort ally. His voice is always insistent
upon that which is first, the righteousness which alone keeps the
mortice and tenon in true. He did not suppose that the marriage
of the *mystique* of the Christian faith to the *mystiques* proper to the
life of the family, to the work of men and women, to civic and
patriotic life, to the monarchy, the republic, and international
relations could ever be anything but charged with difficulties and
tensions of a heartbreaking severity. His own marriage, like
Kierkegaard's broken engagement, wrote in his flesh the price of
such things. Nevertheless he was prepared to take Christ at his
word, to risk all things for the sake of *fidélité* and the promise of
grace. It was because he hungered so passionately for the salvation of France that he spared nothing in the cost of the spiritual
approfondissement without which the crucial issues that posed the
Deuteronomic choice could not ever be seen for what they were.

If the note of such concern sounds unfamiliar to us now, let us
look at one example drawn from more recent times. In his book
on the work of Buber entitled *The Wanderer and the Way*, Roy

Oliver cites Buber's concern for the Zionist State. 'Unlike those lofty idealists who do not lower their gaze below the horizon, Buber never forgot that the immediate challenge was always relations with one's neighbours. In political context that meant the Arabs.' Buber did not compromise. Step by step he insisted on seeking Jewish-Arab co-operation. Defeated, he made clear the nature of the Jerusalem Ideological Conference. Buber wrote:

> Behind everything Ben-Gurion had said on that point there lies, it seems to me, the will to make the political factor supreme. He is one of the proponents of that kind of secularization which cultivates its thoughts and visions so diligently that it keeps men from hearing the voice of the living God. This secularization takes the form of an exaggerated 'politicization'. This politicization of life here strikes at the very spirit itself. The spirit with all its thoughts and visions descends and becomes a function of politics.

Politicization is what Péguy meant by *politique*, the corruption of the vision and huckstering with it, often under the guise of a false *mystique* that parodies the thing it names. *Politique* is always most dangerous when thus presented. The exploitation of such things is evident in the White Man's Burden, in Race, Blood and Soil, in the American Way of Life, in the great Proletarian State. In the British scene today contesting forms of *politique* are no less obvious. The time we live in nevertheless calls for more deliberate spiritual engagement, for the *approfondissement* that was the focus of all the effort that Péguy made. *Approfondissement* may be described as the scouring out at ever deeper and deeper levels of the channels of grace. The terrain through which they are to pass is the political-social-economic workaday life of the world. 'Our invincible fidelity, our youthful fidelity to Christian morals, to Christian poverty, to the deepest lessons of the Gospels, our obstinate, our altogether natural fidelity moving secretly within us, constitute an invisible parish.' The *mystique* of the world recovered as a parish is no bad image to be inspired by in the days of the proclamation of the Global Village.

4

SPIRITUALITY AND ALIENATION

> The convulsions of our English Church itself,
> grievous as they are, seem to be nothing beside
> the danger of its calm and unobtrusive alienation
> in thought and spirit from the great silent multi-
> tude of Englishmen, and again of alienation
> from fact and love of fact – mutual alienations
> both.
>
> F. J. A. HORT 1882

The danger to which Hort referred is in no way lessened but rather concealed by our modern dexterity in handling the themes of alienation and spirituality; because we talk about them lengthily, we may deceive ourselves into supposing that we take them seriously. We drop their names to show how much we are acquainted with them, how conversant we are with both sociological and theological trends or trendiness. Whether we know what these things mean in terms of flesh and blood, in the lives of men and women, churched or unchurched, is another matter. Insistent hammering at the theme provokes a character-istic riposte about the danger of forgetting 'the vertical dimen-sion'. This has its truth but the use made of it is often dubious. It savours of the retort courteous and spares us the unpleasant-ness of the countercheck quarrelsome. But do we know a spiri-tuality that wrestles with the appalling consequences of that alienation to which Hort directed our attention nearly a century ago, and that of that much greater and more far-reaching alien-ation of which Marx wrote still earlier? That the Gifford Lectures by Arend Van Leeuwen, *Critique of Heaven and Earth* should spell out for us the Marxist preception of the 'break between an age-old Christian and a coming post-Christian civilization' is all to the good but we still have to work out what all this means for the approach to prayer which we must make. Just how shall we come before the Lord? Just what have we to remember on the way?

Spirituality is concerned with seeking out what is real in human life. The Christian understanding of this quest, inspired, activated and sustained by a faith in the incarnate Lord, sees it as a penetration into all the conditions and circumstances of life in the world, a learning to see all things in their true light – the light thrown upon them by the light of Christ. The spectrum of this light includes all those various manifestations which the arts, the sciences and other human activities have learned to distinguish. It is the same Lord who is being sought out in and through them all. Spirituality, at its richest, utilizes them all, unifying and relating them in such concord as it comes to be able to achieve, the concordant discord that St Francis de Sales described and which R. C. Zaehner took as his title for a study of the interdependence of faiths.

Such spirituality, in direction Godward, in impetus God-given, turns, not away from, but towards, the created world and human experience in the working out of its response to God. It conceives the Incarnation to be, in Atitzer's words, 'an active and forward-moving process – a process that even now is making all things new'. It sets itself to be attentive to this process, watching and praying to discern the signs and features of it so that the world scene with all its terrifying problems becomes nevertheless the place where men and women meet God. It is so easy to say this and so difficult to realize it that we need to be disciplined and self-critical at all points. The biblical insight into such spirituality so often takes the form of direct and searching interrogation of human beings by God. This is what judgement means: the ceaseless questioning of the temporal by the eternal, and the sifting out and rejection of all that fails to contribute to that incarnational process. This too is strangely perplexing, for God's ways are not our ways, and the evil that we do often appears to pass unchecked, to the dismay of the faithful, whose faith is thereby put to the test of holding on until he vindicates his purpose. There are no short cuts, no slick resolvings of awkward passages, in this revelation of what God is about in our time.

Tension, then, is an inescapable feature of our spirituality and no one was more insistent upon this than von Hügel. 'Christianity', he wrote, 'can and does develop in man a temper, a state of soul, which so deeply and delicately, so sharply and steadily perceives and feels the difference between Time and Eternity, the Fleeting and the Abiding, Pleasure and Beatitude, the Contingent and the Final, the Greatness and God, as to make souls incapable of being paid off in these deepest matters with anything but the genuine coin.' It can and does. Therein certainly lies our hope, but the words drive us back to consider how observant we are, how spiritually sensitive, to be able to know the genuine from the false coin in day-to-day living. What does alienation mean if not that living apart from the realities of our condition as children of God, and living apart for so long that we lose the knowledge of truth? Those fed on substitutes and toxic things are not so healthily hungry that they search for the food of eternal life before all else. Alienation from the light of life can produce an acceptance of fog and filthy air, an acquiescence in pollution. But von Hügel continues: 'No doubt this world-fleeing movement will have to be alternated with, will have to find its stimulus and material in, a world-seeking movement; and only the two together, in their proper proportions and inter-penetrations will furnish the complete service of God by complete mankind.... How much decency, leisure and pay is the sinner to have, till he is helped to love prayer and the thought of God?'

The question was not one that figured very prominently in the disputes and discussions on the pay and conditions of miners or any other groups of workers at that time (1922). Nor did it confront one in the books on prayer that were usually provided for churchgoers. It may be recalled that on one occasion at a joint meeting of coal miners and miners' leaders, a coal owner inquired with heavy sarcasm whether the representatives of the men would like to begin the proceedings with a hymn. The element of dialogue which we have learned to associate with spirituality had not yet appeared to offer a contrast or even a challenge to the assumption at work in the encounters that then took place. Men and women negotiated in the world of alienation from whatever position of power they believed themselves to possess. Power has always corrupted, and power for a very long time had been in the hands of the employer and the financier. Despite the slow growth of social welfare, there seemed to be no likelihood of handling the questions that then arose upon any other basis than that of power. The miners in 1926 were forced back to work on the terms their employers thought fit to offer them. It was nobody's business to answer von Hügel's question. In the world of alienation it could hardly be heard at all.

Fifty years later we may ask ourselves how much we have learned since then that might help us to answer it now. It is interesting to note in René Voillaume's latest address on Christian vocation, that the deep love of Marx for an alienated humanity is commended, and his understanding of what had to be faced is found to be wanting. Perhaps we may consider it no small gain in the approach to our question that something more than a frightened denunciation of Marx has at last become possible for some Christians. Whether we find ourselves better placed to set out the Christian affirmations about the necessities of human life in the world today and to watch and pray in relation to them is another matter. The power struggle has changed its form in the intervening half-century but it has not become less horrific or less destructive of human life. We begin to see that the miners von Hügel mentioned include the miners of gold in the Union of South Africa, of copper in Zambia, of tin and tungsten and scores of other materials around the world, but the question remains, and if we don't like the spectre that Marx spoke of we might profitably treat von Hügel's question as something to be embraced rather than exorcized or ignored. In any case it won't go away until the matter of alienation has been faced.

The trouble about playing the power game is that it teaches the players to learn a winners-take-all mentality. Torture and violence and terrorism take on a new lease of life in the midst of a highly sophisticated culture. The newcomers to the struggle learn fast because survival often depends upon it. When we find this disquieting we might reflect on Browning's lines: 'Who taught the dog that trick you hang him for?' I write this because there is a temptation specially designed for the world-renouncers, indeed for all of us who don't want to be involved in the mire of the conflict in politics and economics and ideologies, the temptation to try to plead pre-occupation with other, sometimes called 'more spiritual' things. We can make a fair bid to do these other things well, and it can't be said that they aren't worth doing. 'These ye ought to have done.' But at what cost? At whose expense? It is possible for a few to live in voluntary poverty in the midst of a highly developed affluent economy and to devote their lives to the vision of God and to works of charity. It is most desirable that such 'minimal living' should be set deliberately over against the raucous glorification of increasing per capita incomes. Such voluntarism may well be a much needed gesture on the part of Christians. But the question we have still to ask concerns not the few but the many, the many who must work in this field where the power game prevails and on whose work continuing we all depend. Our relation to these men and women cannot be a negative one only. We owe them too much for that. Dickens, who had an unerring eye for such things, has left us the figure of Harold Skimpole whose affection for the simple things of life made simplicity itself a sublimely selfish affectation. All of us can assume so easily that someone will empty the dust bins in great cities, or keep power stations running or work throughout the night on half a hundred jobs. And what, asks von Hügel, of their spirituality?

We can only begin to answer the question by a radical examination of the possibilities of genuine communication between those alienated from each other, from their handiwork, from their essential selves, and from nature. Anything else means bargaining with counters and many of these we know to be spurious. 'To be radical', wrote Marx, 'is to go to the root of the question. Now the root of mankind is man.' We have to learn all over again to see The Man. We have to reflect upon that mocking phrase 'Behold the Man' and see him in him or her who stands in our midst alone, despised, hated, mocked and rejected.

We have to ponder upon the kind of rejection which goes on all the time in our own society.

A spirituality that takes seriously the kind and extent of alienation – are we not all aliens today? ... that has prevailed with increasing power during the past three hundred years must needs pay greater attention than has been our custom to what von Hügel called 'the life prior to prayer', to those actual conditions in which men and women live and to the questions which these conditions should prompt in the minds of those who believe in an incarnational theology. The bruised, the maimed, the blinded, the starved, the oppressed are everywhere about us, and in each and all of them the Son of Man is degraded and rejected anew. Christian spirituality does not begin by separating Martha and Mary but by seeing that both have work to do. The miner, says von Hügel is still there to remind us of this.

5

SOME INTIMATIONS OF SPIRITUALITY

I have chosen this title for several reasons. On so vast and awesome a subject as spirituality it would be most fitting to begin by remembering one's own limitations, and even though feeling deeply about it, not to speak in those over-familiar terms with which, I fear, clergymen have all too often offended the laity of both sexes. Whatever else it may be it is not clerical property, nor even a subject which is better known by virtue of ordination. It appeared to demand the kind of approach which a gentle portmanteau word like 'intimation' announced. The word itself has meant many things. The *Oxford English Dictionary* lists some like 'formal notification, stern requirement, hint and suggestion' and it carries something personal, guessed at rather than fully perceived, a resonance, a summons, an invitation, and in that last resort a humbled acknowledgement of

> The incumbent mystery of sense and soul
> Of life and death, time and eternity.

All in all, a very Wordsworthian word.

As such it seemed appropriate to spirituality itself, as being the area of response that human beings discover and speak about on their becoming aware of God. They come to it in all sorts of ways, through disclosures of pain and delight, through being moved by hopes and desires, through being addressed by unforeseen things, through sudden syntheses of hitherto chaotic pieces and no less unexpected fractures of one-time impregnable things, all revealing what one artist described as a 'splendid gratuitousness' and one evangelist as 'grace', in which we are called to delight, not as onlookers only, but as recipients of, and participants in, its costliness and its glory.

It is then with intimations that I want to begin, such

41

intimations as to the nature of the spirituality which we should be concerned with today, as I, limited as I am, feel have reached me. There must be a wealth of others, and our interchange now must supply the deficiencies of this awareness of mine. Let me indicate briefly something of their extent. We have to do in these days increasingly with what must be seen as one world, have to realize that admitting to first, second and third worlds is, while realistic, also a prescription for world disaster. The spirituality which acknowledges one God one Father of all cannot tolerate, if it be true to itself, the flagrant denials of this in practice and theory in political and economic relations of the world's peoples. Its business is not to devise blue-prints for re-ordered society, but to affirm as clearly as possible the demands of justice and mercy, of the 'fairness' which Simone Weil spent so much of her passionate short life in declaring, of the righteousness which Jewish scriptures extended to matters of human dignity, and a respect for human freedom. Spirituality must be by nature prophetic in the sense that it regards what God will be doing in time, time at hand, and time to come, because, as Blake said, 'Eternity is in love with the productions of Time.'

Secondly, any further extension of this spirituality must have an environmental sensitivity, reminding men and women that because they are of the earth compounded, and dependent upon it, they not only misuse it at their peril, but dishonour God who placed them in it. The sad degeneration of the word 'exploitation' is witness to a whole process of recklessness in misusing the earth and its people. A new look at the ground we stand on is always a 'must' if we are to know ourselves in the presence of God in the factory, laboratory, farm and city, all of which have their particular problems of right usage and ultimate purpose.

Spirituality here then takes on the character of a constant critique of human behaviour in all places whatsoever and it is woefully true that we have, in Lear's words, 'ta'en too little care of this' for too long a time. I look out daily at Sellafield, an establishment which is in so many ways instrumental to an image of things to come. Its perimeter fences constantly being extended, the ubiquitous police, its lavish expenditure, and the secrecy which surrounds it are an uncanny manifestation of that city of the future which Rex Warner described years ago in his novel *The Wild Goose Chase*. It compels one to ask whether this be the up-to-date Tower of Babel, being built even bigger and more lofty in purpose, presaging disaster, or the city spared as yet for the sake of ten righteous within it. Our eyes must be turned no less both on inner cities and suburbia. Suburbia where our churches, if the word 'flourish' may still be used, do that; inner cities where the heroic efforts of both men and women to bear witness to God are washed over with tides of squalor and hopelessness, violence and unallayed hungers. Perhaps the most telling imagery of our time in respect of our inner cities is that its sewage system is approaching breakdown. Spirituality might well pray for God to send us not just another Chadwick but churches possessed of a vision and commitment to life that faces as he did the task set by such conditions. Need I extend this to the whole countryside, to the rivers and seas, the forests and soil of the entire world?

Thirdly, human relationships spell out our spiritual tasks and our many failures. I shall put the sexual ones first as most basic to the shaping of human life. Now there has been great gain in the last fifty years, enough to make us rejoice. Every day, none the less, there is that which should make us weep. All too evident still is the truth of Lawrence's phrase, 'We are crucified by sex.' I am thinking less of the sexual misdemeanours and more of the failure to work out a deepened knowledge of adult sexuality, to set forward the search for the sacred in sexual relations, not mainly in procreation but in new understanding of conjugal love; such love can neither be planned nor managed, it can only be nurtured, and this, not by being turned in on itself, but understood and valued as the socially most important area of human education. Jack Dominian says that if people today find Christianity irrelevant to their lives it is because 'Christianity has failed in its fundamental mission which is to be the catalyst of Love to the world.' This area of life called sexual is so taut and strained by fear and confusion and ignorance that almost more than anything else it warps and distorts both our feelings and relations to others. Here, but not only here, as Rowan Williams has insisted, 'spirituality becomes far more than a science of interpreting exceptional private experiences; it must now touch every area of human experience, the public and social, the painful, negative, even pathological byways of the mind, the moral and relational world.' He continues, 'The goal of a Christian life becomes not enlightenment but wholeness, an acceptance of this complicated and muddled bundle of experience as a possible theatre for God's creative work.'

This is by no means the only area in which the dread fact of what we have learned to call alienation has to be faced. The word has no doubt become a cliché, more dangerous in so doing, but let us remember that more than a century ago Marx pointed to the degrees of alienation of human beings from their work, from other people, from nature and from themselves which were built into the fabric of daily life, and F. J. A. Hort as a sensitive churchman warned his fellow Anglicans of the alienation of the Church itself from 'the great silent multitude of Englishmen, and again of alienation from fact and love of fact – mutual alienations both.' Dare we say, as we look at the working life of our nation today or the Church's position in English society that the warnings of either of these have been taken to heart? Does not the fact of alienation show itself in the crude violence that everyday now excites comment? But for spirituality the matter does not stop there. Browning's awkward question, 'Who taught the dog the trick you hang him for?' remains to be answered by all of us who do not want to be too closely involved in this mire and turn to what are more so-called spiritual things. Spirituality cannot be content with negative relations to men and women, because its charter is that of love, a love that requires us to seek that which is meaningful in human affairs, along roads which we have not passed heretofore, and which therefore demand of us more and more self-giving effort.

Fourthly, I would try to face what is at stake in ecumenicity, towards which with much grudging and coolness Christian churches have moved. We have cause to rejoice that so much has been done. As I tried to prepare for this paper there reached me from various parts of the world and different churches vivid intimations of the Spirit at work: many facets of what has been well described as 'the tension between the imperfect soul and the magnetic perfection which is conceived of as lying beyond it', being followed up by courageous and trustful movements towards reconciliation and more concerted life. I took up a book *Vamos Caminando* (Let us go forward), a recently published cate-chetical programme from Peru, opening with a plea to us old-world Christians to have 'courage and goodwill to recognize in the simple Good News from the Andes, the voice of God's Spirit speaking through the new poor of Yahweh.' I turned then to bulletins of work being done in the Tamil Rehabilitation Centre, prison work, in the South Indian diocese of Madurai-Ramned and in the small villages where the struggle with disease, oppression, crime and poverty is intense. A third voice came through Vincent Donovan's hauntingly searching and beautiful epistle, as he calls it, from the Masai. Yet another came from re-reading Bishop Ting's reflections on the state of the Church in China, in what he described as 'a post-denominational, post-ultra-leftish' situation. These and many others sketched out the dimensions of ecumenicity.

In all this were well-known things mingled with new ones. Von Hügel taught my generation to think of rich spiritual life in terms of confluence: the running together of a great many streams, not all of them bearing Christian names. Today the panorama is wider, and we are conscious of some polluted streams and explosive situations which honest spirituality cannot ignore. It compels us to see that what we most prize in the spiritual life is not a private possession, and that moreover like the manna that was not daily renewed, it goes rotten when not re-directed anew by outgoing vision. Ecumenicity may help it to be healthy if we can learn to see it as a kind of Mandala table of spiritual elements whose variety and singular properties as well as their givenness in the creation promises ever richer results to wise handling. Having made some progress in learning to see what possibilities God has set before us in this wealth of gases and liquids and metals and the incredible complexities of their interactions and combinations, we may be a little more fitted to deal humbly and wisely with human elements no less complex, and to accept responsibility for our fellow human beings and the life of the world through the channels of prayer and common life. Paying attention to such things is the preliminary aspect of all valid prayer, just as honesty of purpose is essential to it. Ecumenicity is a step towards a genuine catholicity which the Christian Church has since its earliest days recognized as one of its true marks, as well as a reminder to each and all of us that the whole truth is not the private possession of some by right of entail.

Before going further I want to add a fifth intimation of what our spirituality must be greatly concerned with always. The Gospels, indeed the whole Bible, relate this attentiveness of life of a Godward kind, to concern for the sick, the maimed, the deprived, not as proof of its powers, not as a way of meritorious living, but as an integral part of spiritual discernment and response. 'I was an hungered and ye gave me no meat: I was thirsty, and ye gave me no drink: I was a stranger, and ye took me not in: naked, and ye clothed me not: sick and in prison and ye visited me not' (Matthew 25.42–3). This is not the time to protest that Christians have done much good work in these fields, for spirituality sensitive to the human condition can make no claims beyond those of a penitent plea to be given a chance to do more, to be quickened where it has been lethargic, perceptive where it has been myopic.

I quote here from a novel of Albert Camus, *La Peste*, its author no friend to conventional pietism, itself one of the most profoundly imaginative portrayals of the human city today. 'I have realized', says one of the sensitive characters in the book, 'that we all have the plague ... and that one must do what one can to cease being plague-stricken, to keep endless watch on ourselves lest in a careless moment we breathe into somebody's face and fasten the infection on him.' I do not need, I am sure, to expand the infection, it has touched all aspects of human life, including our speaking one to another. 'What interests me,' the Camus character continues, 'is learning how to become a saint,' saintliness meaning 'the way of total compassion', to which it would not be ill-judged to add words from the Epistle to the Ephesians, 'till we all come in the unity of faith ... to the measure of the stature of the fullness of Christ.'

Sanctification has a long, honourable place in the history of spirituality, and while we may sometimes find earlier conceptions of what sanctity meant embarrassing, even repulsive, we acknowledge, I think, that it points to something important which we have to take trouble to retain in our grammar of spirituality and learn to give a much wider range of reference. (I knew a gentleman once who referred to *Crockford* as 'my book of saints' which I considered excessive!) In an age which is anti-heroic there is a great deal to be said for unashamedly conversing with those men and women, nameless and named, who have glorified God and made the world something more fragrant because they have lived.

I would link this up with Martin Buber's life-long insistence on our spiritual task of becoming aware of the other person as person, a thou to our I, which is how by God's infinite mercy we stand in relation to him. And to make this most pertinent to our time may I quote a short passage from one of von Hügel's addresses in which he asked: 'How much decency, leisure and pay is the miner to have till he is helped to love prayer and the thought of God? Ought not any and every man's mind and conscience to be developed simultaneously with his merely wage-earning activities? Does not that noble large interest in the things that matter in themselves do more to moderate a man's desire for the visible good things of life than all the Acts of parliament that ever were or will be?' The date 1922 (*Essays and Addresses,* 2nd series, p. 272). Must we not say the same for all men and women caught up willy nilly in the processes of production all round the world? It is forty years since Bonhoeffer called on us to see in the Christ we profess to serve 'the man for others', to risk pains and penalties for a commitment of our church life to such purpose. I could wish that it were in the forefront of any discussion of what spirituality means, that we were kept always in range of hearing the question which Michael Wilson asked in his book *Health is for All*: 'At whose expense am I healthy?' Would that we all of us were reminded again and again of the biblical words, 'Where is your brother? Why have you not brought him?' What is it that hinders us here?

*

Permit me at this point to make a slight personal detour to illustrate as much by default as anything else what can or did happen to many like myself in these matters. I would detail it under
three heads.

First, some years ago I assembled as much as I could of
material for writing a book on the Anglican parson portrayed in
novels from the mid-eighteenth century until today: an immense
array of several hundred books. You must forgive me for
confining my attention to the question voiced by Carlyle, 'Him
of the shovel hat, O heavens, what shall we say of him?'
Novelists had in fact a great deal to say of him and with a few
exceptions, it is uniformly depressing, though expressed in
mainly amused satirical fashion. The man, by and large, is a
clown, the Shakespearean fool, not in motley, but in cloth that
seems always to be spoken of with respect, he who wears it with
virtually none. Mainly conceived as a hired talker who gives that
unpleasant word 'sermonizing' to English life, little regarded
and therefore, as Swift observed, sure to be despised, he is by his
most serious and fairest critic, George Eliot, dismissed as the
most irresponsible of all talkers. A few sentimentally pictured
innocents like Parson Primrose and Mr Harding apart, the
cavalcade which begins with the Shuffles, the Snuffles and
Thwackums of eighteenth-century coarseness, which replaces
them with social climbers and parson-magistrates in the Jane
Austen, Brontë, Thackeray world, and closes the nineteenth century with acid remarks from Meredith and Hardy, leaves the
reader in little doubt about the absence of a spiritual dimension.

Was that just a picture? Or shall we say, with Bernard
Blackstone's remark in mind about Virginia Woolf's dismissal of
clergymen as lacking any fine sense of values, as having attained
no pearl of great price, that neither Grub Street nor Bloomsbury
were in a position to make right judgements about them? The
truth is, I believe, that English society, devastatingly secularized
under the last of the Tudors, expected so little in spiritual terms
from a church which had become quite remote from the great
mass of the people, that it laughed rather than raged or lamented at its unreal condition. There are some exceptions, but few
people now would read Newman's *Loss and Gain*, Froude's *Nemesis*

of Faith, Disraeli's *Samuel* or even Mrs Humphrey Ward's *Robert Elsmere.* Few people could recall any parson in Dickens who merited that author's approval. For the twentieth-century novelist this institution and its clergy has been little more than a quaint survival and the English have a taste for such things. What was missing was any deep sense of holiness, of conflict between powers of light and darkness, such as, for example, we find in the work of a novelist like Bernanos.

Second, I look at my own experience of being ordained something over fifty years ago, and the training, if such a word could be used, which I then received for ministry in the established Church. It occurred midway between the two wars when one might have presumed that in sorrow and penitence renewed effort to hear and act upon what the Spirit might have to say to the churches would have been uppermost on the agenda. There had been before the Great War was ended a National Mission of Repentance and Hope. There had been some prophets like Studdert Kennedy, there were some teachers exercised to rediscover the relevance of Christianity to the contemporary world. This was the time when Evelyn Underhill wrote: 'Enrichment of the sense of God is the crying need of current Christianity.' That cry did not greatly disturb us, and though much serious work was done through conferences to relate Christian faith to the social, economic and political aspects of current life, it was Prayer-Book revision and contraception which hogged most attention. My training consisted of lectures in Doctrine, Church History, Biblical Studies, and a routine of offices in chapel. After four terms I was ordained, the sole deacon on that occasion, when the preacher, I remember, lamented the poverty of the land. He spoke more aptly than I fancy he guessed.

In all this time, though of course we discussed the doctrine of the Holy Spirit, and charismatic movements had not appeared to trouble our institutional waters, the nature, the history, the commitments of spirituality were never faced. Some spiritual classics, I had, of course read, but they belonged to a terrain one visited like going abroad. T. S. Eliot revived an interest in Lancelot Andrewes and Jacobean piety in Little Gidding and Bemerton, but these were literary excursions. I can still faintly

recall my astonishment when I first read Bede Frost's little book
on mental prayer it was like 'straying onto the shores of that
immortal sea, which brought us hither,' and hearing 'the voice of
many waters of mighty thunderings saying Alleluia, for the Lord
God omnipotent reigneth,' and then one went home again.

Third, ordination meant several things. I was now one of
'them' of whom the novelists said those hard things: separated
from the laity, appointed and paid to minister to them on terms
which to them were not greatly different from those which governed the medical or legal profession. I was favoured by being
relieved from the pressures of having to find a house and a job,
which affected the lives of most other men and women, but my
relationships with them were awkwardly defined. To the great
majority I was simply a representative of an institution which
they occasionally used, beyond which I filled in my time in some
unknown fashion. The little girl who stopped me in the street
one day and asked me if I was God I had to disillusion; adults
did not need it.

I was immersed in the chores of a parish, a round of social,
pastoral, liturgical duties. It was nobody's business but my own
to relate these things to spirituality, and though I made use of
some retreats to try to learn more about praying, these too were
separated from the life of parishioners, and offered little
foothold to anyone wanting to find a way into the depth of it or
its further reaches which was where the language of my profession indicated I should be, that is to say, where salvation, holiness, the nature of God and the Christ were, along with prayer,
of primary concern. It was, in rock-climbing terms, an awkward
traverse which separated us, and how or what to communicate
appeared ever more difficult.

I was discovering at first hand what is evident enough to
others, that spirituality, even the word, was repugnant to many.
Quite recently a reviewer in the *Times Literary Supplement* began
by expressing his dislike for what he called 'pious practices',
something which he regarded no doubt as escapist, élitist, pietis-
tic, unreal! They are not so obtrusive in English life as to excite
more than distaste, but I recall the slightly shocked looks on the
faces of some attending the Parker enquiry into the nuclear

industry when they found a Buddhist monk sitting on the pavement engaged in prayer! They suspected subversion!

Was the language the problem? The people I lived amongst were as conscious of suffering and death, of love and hatred, of guilt and resentment, of terror and grief, as I was, but how did these things figure in a shared mode of life in practice? The foreground of daily life in Barrow-in-Furness at the time was rearmament for the Second World War; in West Cumberland it was the almost total unemployment producing a hopelessness approaching despair. Where did 'enrichment of the sense of God', desperately needed, find access there? My prolonged education had not greatly helped me, some might have said it had actually unfitted me, to answer that question. My job as parish priest was to maintain as some kind of going concern the activities of the Church whose vitality would for many, be measured in terms of numbers and money. Its relevance to a world in which the Holocaust and Hiroshima were being prepared for was anything but clear.

I think I must curtail this personal reflection, or rather turn it at this stage to consideration of what it led me to, fumbling and greatly perplexed. Of the business of the Church to be, that I had not the slightest doubt; but the shape was wrong, its mode of living was wrong, its methods wasteful and misdirected, because spirituality as I began to see it was not the thing it was primarily concerned with nor able to nourish.

What spirituality meant to me was what I found years later in the title of John MacMurray's Swarthmore Lectures (1965) *Search for Reality in Religion*, when religion means the behaviour of the entirely whole man or woman and the reflection upon it which sanctifies and gives meaning to it in the context of the universe and its history, a search which for some of us had its roots in the Judaic-Christian tradition.

The trouble with the Church as I saw it was that it had stopped searching in any determined fashion. It gave the impression that it knew the answers to all human problems, whereas it had actually been keeping its head down or dodging most of them. It was not in any case geared to deal with them. Feedback from people's experience of living and the questioning that this did provoke (in some minds at least) into acts of meditation and prayer, oblation, consecration and communion was not purposeful and generous enough to provide the spiritual diet that was needed. All too much of what it offered was, in Pauline terms, milk for babes; on sexual matters it was pre-pubertal or encapsulated in procreation; in working life, which by the simple machinery of clocking-on and shifts, governed most people's lives, it had hardly begun to understand what sort of world this was. Its imagery was still pastoral, patriarchal, metaphysical, so that its symbolic language failed to describe or illuminate or give religious meaning to what human beings in the twentieth century were engaged in doing. It was being edged out of living affairs by slogans, by doctrines devised for the market, by crude popularizations of the laws of thermodynamics. Worse still, it offered no adequate channels for the preparation for prayer which long ago Jewish teachers had realized to be all-important. It did not assemble its members to speak to each other as very members of the Body of Christ, so that it left them a prey to the individualism whose falsehoods are the most deadly temptations besetting our world, infecting its prayer and its sacramental life …

I was, much later in life, interested in MacMurray's pilgrimage from the birthplace in Scottish Calvinism through various denominations and the Student Christian Movement to the point where, as still a young man, he abjured membership of any religious body, though professing and teaching the Christian faith, until in old age he joined the Society of Friends. He wrote of that step: 'Our human being is our relation to other human beings: our relation to God is itself real only as it shows itself in our relation to our neighbours.' He valued the very name Friends, as being that which Jesus himself had used. I did not opt out of denominational membership, perhaps because I had more opportunity as priest to try to do what I believed in through membership of the Church, and because I attached more importance to the historic Catholic tradition. The English are very susceptible to the temptation to play Robinson Crusoe in this as in other things. What I did try to do as regards

reshaping the life of the local church and my own efforts to pray,
I want now very briefly to speak of.

What has the search for reality in religion meant in my very
limited understanding and practice of it?

First, a recognition of and readiness to pay attention to what
I call intimations, things which overtake one in unpredictable
ways, not always in spectacular fashion like being cornered by
the Hound of Heaven; much more in what Wordsworth called
'yearnings, misgivings, obstinate questionings' and the like,
which he came to recognize as renovating, repairing, and nourishing, making

> Our noisy years seem moments in the being
> Of the eternal silence.

However fugitive and uncontrollable one's own responses to
these moments might be it meant making room for silence alone
or in the company of others.

Second, though this is in practice the first step, preparation
for prayer which is not to be jumped into. When Hamlet said,

> For every man hath business and desire,
> Such as it is – and for mine own poor part,
> Look you, I'll go pray,
>
> Hamlet i.v.130–2

what did he intend by that, and what should we? It meant more
than 'thinking things out', more than seeking for what appear to
be satisfactory solutions to our problems – important as these
must be, because in this business of prayer it is with God, infinite
and eternal, the personally conceived Reality with whom we
have to do: not a problem to be solved, but a relationship to
be discerned and honoured, most truly expressed in terms of
loving.

Such prayer begins rightly with a desire, at once humble and
omnivorous, 'Give me an understanding heart,' where heart
means mind, will, feelings and imagination, the totality of our
being. It seeks to know more in the sense of being more united
with God. Its knowledge matures not in blind or resigned

acceptance of what appears to be true, or in what in frightened or arrogant moods it wants to be true, but in the pressing of questions which it is minded to ask because only so does it honour him who is more than all it can ever know, but whom it approaches in free and fearless loving with questions because he has made himself open to them. It is an ongoing relationship, to be discerned in every part or particle of the universe that is both the foundation and achievement of such praying and loving. You may remember Meredith's lines:

> Ah what a dusty answer gets the soul,
> When hot for certainties in this our life!

The poem in telling us that these lovers:

> ... fed not on the advancing hours:
> Their hearts held cravings for the buried day,

indicates why. Asking the right questions in the right spirit is also the task of learning to pray as it is of learning to live in love. Compounded of all our creaturely cries of need, distress, delight and wonder, whether voiced or silent, it puts its questions in a confidence begotten by love. It addresses him, the Silent One, in the strength of its yearning to respond to the love by which it has been begotten. It numbers its days not with unsatisfied cravings or regrets, but with a growing assurance of infinite richness.

Such questioning touches internal springs from every aspect of life of which it has any experience. Fundamental to it is a sense of the creation, to establish a right relationship with the cosmos which it believes to be the object of God's love. Spirituality learns to regard it in terms of speech – God said – but as Martin Buber has taught us to think of it, not as speech rushing over our heads, but speech directed precisely at us. It seeks to be known, as a gift may be said to do, to bring the giver and him to whom it is given into deeper bonds of love.

This applies no less to history, the reality of which consists in 'the mutual presence of God and man in the conscious creation of the world.' We have, I think, much too readily talked of God's plan for the world, too easily presumed to set it out for a programme to be carried out. But God, whose concern for the freedom in which love is born is absolute, is not a divine puppeteer. Human history must exhibit that freedom, the choice set out so clearly by the Deuteronomic writer: 'I have set before you life and death, blessing and cursing, therefore choose life, that both thou and thy seed may live, that thou mayest love the Lord thy God' (Deuteronomy 30.18). Human history must likewise afford that distillation of spiritual experience which gives an increasing reality to the choices that have to be made. It is one of the chief functions of historical inquiry to dethrone the idols that otherwise obstruct this freedom, to dispel the fantasies that the fearful are inclined to give way to. It applies furthermore to theology which if it be not liberating from all idolatries including those of its own construction, is not honest-to-God who loves his creatures.

It seems to me then that the spirituality we seek is not that of either laity or religious, but that of the one holy people of God, a thing in which we have not hitherto made much way. It will be concerned to replace those sometime exclusive walls that have divided men and women into denominational groups and churches over against the non-churched, by something more like a sensitive skin which registers contact and communication of pain and delight. We have made a start towards this. There is a great deal of pain to be faced ahead, and it may well be that Christians have not yet, in their spirituality, learned to exercise that great solvent of rigidities, God's gift of laughter.

We shall do these things with goodwill and good sense only if we see the task with a much more adequate sense of our common humanity. The gross scandals of the divisions of freemen and slaves, rich and poor, men and women, advantaged and disadvantaged, have in spite of the prophets and saints attended Christian society throughout its history. We read Amos and James but we do not always honour their words, and our spirituality lapses into more unreality than we care to admit – as a consequence of our default. It is fatally easy to respond 'Let our cry come unto thee,' and be quite oblivious to the cries of those in our very midst on whom burdens of hardship, deprivation and despair are placed. True spirituality requires recognition of them, a willingness on our part and for their sake to enter, in Péguy's words, 'the kingdom of incurable anxiety'.

It will be done only so far as our prayer kindles passion. I believe that Unamuno was right in saying that without it we could believe in our concepts and ideas of God, but not in God himself. Rosemary Haughton and others have done well in reminding us that passion is at the heart of Christian faith in both active and passive senses. When the long imbalance in human society of the two sexes begins to be replaced by an honouring of the divine gifts to both, it will be for women to teach men how to be passionate, yet gentle and quiet in spirit, empowered by passion yet not possessed by it.

All this does in fact demand a new language, a new mode of communication among human beings, between humanity and God, beginning with a more deliberate recognition of our need for poets, musicians and artists of every kind, so inadequately used during the past three centuries. Something which Coleridge among others was pleading for almost two hundred years ago, both in terms of a wider clerisy and of the nature and work of imagination is at long last beginning to be more commonly accepted. A religious consciousness is nurtured by those symbolic forms and acts used in the arts which relate human beings to the ultimate truths of their existence. 'The artist is the man who goes into the empty space,' wrote Hillis Miller (and I am not sure of that word 'empty') 'between man and God, and takes the enormous risk of attempting to create in that vacancy a new fabric of connections between man and the divine power.' To do this requires the most vigorous imagination, of which Coleridge said that it brought the whole human soul into activity and ordered experience, so that it became a coherent whole.

It was never more necessary in human history to essay to do this: the alternative to symbolism that can effect it is a diabolism which brings all things to chaos. We are even now still living in the aftermath of an experience that has wrung from our lips the anguished words, 'No poetry after Auschwitz'. Our human integrity is at stake in the language we use. The poet's task is to make new what has been defaced, clean what has been defiled, bring to joy what has been well-nigh drowned in its tears. 'Set a

watch, O Lord before my mouth: and keep the doors of my lips'
(Psalm 14.3). I have no space to say more: but may I repeat some
words that say more than I could ever hope to do, however much
space were allowed. They are the words of a young impassioned
lover:

> What you do
> Still betters what is done. When you speak, sweet,
> I'd have you do it ever; when you sing,
> I'd have you buy and sell so, so give alms,
> Pray so; and for the ord'ring your affairs,
> To sing them too. When you do dance, I wish you
> A wave o' th' sea, that you might ever do
> Nothing but that still, move still, still so,
> And own no other function.
>
> *The Winter's Tale* iv.iv.135–43

Would not Love Divine, the lover of all humankind, say as much
and more of each and all whom he loves? Is it not the task of
spirituality to hear what he says and how he says it, and share it
with others?

6

ON PRAYING

'If you want your daughter's company, you must shorten your steps and walk slowly; else she will lose her breath in her desire to keep up with you.' So wrote Fr George Tyrrell to that wise great teacher of spiritual truths, Baron von Hügel. It was necessary counsel, accepted and valued, so that in a great deal of von Hügel's later writing there is a note of anxiety lest the teacher overburden the pupil and destroy what he hoped to nourish.

The warning needs to be reflected upon and heeded if what follows here is not to be dismissed as too elementary to be much help in this matter of praying. What is here suggested springs from a conviction that we cannot be too short in our steps in setting out to help ourselves and others to pray. It begins therefore at the simplest level because the people to whom it is offered are those who find it very difficult to walk this way at all, much less keep up with those who stride, or appear to stride, confidently and quickly along its roads.

It begins in this way because on all sides people are to be heard saying, when honest speaking about prayer is going on, that they do not pray, do not know how to pray, do not know where to turn for help, do not know how to keep going with it in ways they once used. They say these things ruefully, apologetically, sadly, indicating a sense of need, a sense of loss, a sense of guilt, and all this, strangely enough, when aids to prayer, manuals of devotion, and the counsels of the great masters of the spiritual life are easily available. Why, then, the continuing admissions of frustration? Is it not possible that, given all the special circumstances of life in the world today, so much of the help traditionally offered begins at a point beyond the reach of very many people or leaves them breathless?

What follows is divided into two parts. The first plunges into the practice of praying with some suggestions about beginning to pray. *On s'engage et puis on voit.* The second is intended to help you to reflect about the business of praying and to see a little more clearly what kind of thing we are doing when we set out to pray. You may be inclined to disagree with these reflections, but even so they may provoke you to think out for yourself more satisfactory convictions. This plan has been followed because the impulse or desire to pray very often breaks into our conscious-ness and at that point we need help to act quickly, deliberately and surely. Thereafter we need another kind of help which both deals with the questioning that praying itself provokes and gives us some working basis for going on with it more systematically.

BEGINNING TO PRAY

There are three commonly experienced moments in everyday living which can be used as the beginning of praying: three moments which seem by their very nature to prompt us to pray.

1 When we feel glad, grateful, pleased, relieved, exhilarated, joyful etc.
2 When we feel the need for help: when we are frightened, anxious, distressed, in pain, perplexed, etc.
3 When we are tired to the point of exhaustion – flat out, beaten, etc.

The moment of gladness

The simplest thing that we can do when we come to this moment is to say 'Thank you.' We should say this straight-forwardly to someone who has given us something or done something for us. The glad moment is the recognition of some-thing given or done, and the right response on our part is grati-tude. The praying is simply saying, 'Thank you for that.'

It is obvious that many people do this spontaneously, saying, 'Thank God for that,' and they vary a good deal in the implica-tions they give to using the word God. If you are used to using 'God', go on doing so, but if not, simply say 'Thank you' and leave the 'you' to be pondered upon later. The important things is to let the gratitude take hold of you and to surround your experience with gratitude.

'Thank you's' vary in everyday life from a curt perfunctory acknowledgement to a deep awareness of what we have received and an almost overwhelming sense of unworthiness. Our praying 'Thank you' when it is sparked off by a spontaneous moment of gladness, has the potentiality of being deepened, and praying at this point means deliberately prolonging, extending, savouring the expression of gratitude so that it doesn't drop away unused and unexplored. To pray is to make the most of our moments of perception. You pause on the thing that has happened, you turn it over and over like a person examining a gift, you set it in the context of past and future, you mentally draw out its possibilities, you give the moment time to reveal what is embedded in it. As you are doing this you may be saying 'Thank you' many times with your lips or you may be silently following the path of appreciation. It is the deliberate extension of the moment of gratitude which is important, whatever means you employ to bring this about.

What is here prompted by a spontaneous recognition of the good thing encountered now needs to be used as the willed basis for praying when we come to sit down or kneel down to reflect upon a day's experience. It may well be that at no time during the day have we felt glad or has occasion for gratitude been clearly grasped. What we are to do now in our praying is to review that experience and pick out what we can say 'Thank you' for. We are to give gratitude a chance to germinate in the events that have already become our experience.

We shall not learn to do this quickly, nor shall we put ourselves to the trouble of attempting it unless we see how important it is. To have lived through a day and yet not be able to be thankful for one moment of it is to be living a death-in-life. It means that our senses and our faculties are being deadened so that instead of providing us with a rich store of valued experience they are simply enabling us to exist. This was a condition in which a great many human beings were placed in concentration camps by the deliberate act of their persecutors. But what more do we do for ourselves if we fail to make possible the growth of pleasure in, and gratitude for, some part of our daily experience? To learn to sift that experience in a way that picks out more and more that engenders gratitude is what praying is about, and it should be clear from this that such praying is a deep necessity in human life. Without such growth in sensitive awareness of, and thankful response to, the events of potential enrichment, we do in fact die spiritually.

So much then turns upon our willingness to say 'Thank you'. It prompts this simplest act which can be extended in reflective rumination over the whole fabric of our day's experience, growing ever more keen in discrimination and far-sighted in making connections, so that what begins with moments is extended into actual tracts of experience. It is the 'practised eye' which begins to discern what the fabric itself is really like. The old counsel 'Count your many blessings' was right enough so far: what is needed is this growing capability of seeing in things that don't look like blessings at all still deeper occasions for gratitude.

All this has a further frame of reference with regard to other people. We are set to learn to say 'Thank you' not only for our experience but for theirs too. Our praying must take account of other people's lives and enmesh them in this network of gratitude. It can begin on the simplest level of our observation of their moments of gladness and be deliberately pursued in reflective prayer that uses such knowledge as we gain of them to surround them with thankfulness. The kind of prayer called intercession must have its roots in this.

One other point deserves to be noticed here. It is more useful in learning to take these first steps in prayer to leave such questions as 'To whom do we pray?' than to try to sort out our theology of prayer. Walt Whitman addressed his poem to 'You whoever you are' and Leslie Fielder comments: 'Is there an Other to whom one can speak, a real beloved, a real audience, a real God?' In our praying we speak to 'You whoever you are' and mean the Other who is more real than anything else in the Universe. To conceive of the Other in terms of personality is the best we can do, and the gratitude we address to the Other is likewise the best we can offer. It is in the willed deliberate extension of this that we learn more of the Other, and it is far better that we should avoid trying to enclose in fixed terms what we are in process of learning. Much that is most valuable in the arts and literature is chock-full of ambiguities: much that is most important in learning to pray is laid hold of under the same conditions of ambiguity.

The moment of need

Just as people say 'Thank God for that', so too they exclaim 'God help me', meaning much or little in both cases. It is the felt need that is the starting point here and this has a reality for us which we are not in doubt about. If I am frightened I need to be reassured, if I am anxious I need to be relieved, if I am perplexed I need redirection. I may be hazy or even wrong about the causes of my troubles, but the kind of praying we are concerned with here simply expresses my need for help and my belief, hope and expectation that I can be helped. The Syro-Phoenician woman's very straightforward plea 'Lord, help me' is the model for praying in this kind. Again, as with the prayer of thankfulness, it hardly matters whether you repeat 'Help me' in words or whether you silently shape you whole frame of mind to an attitude of supplication for help. The important thing is to grasp and prolong the attitude of the moment and to permit it to become deepened so that the immediate felt need that prompted it is extended to still greater need.

The quality of this may be more clearly grasped if we see the difference between this extended plea for help and the condition of worrying. Our very intention which is to oust anxiety and worry prompts the assertion of something like recognized and accepted dependence on 'You whoever you are'. This kind of praying indeed, like the prayer of gratitude, is a process-affair in which we are to learn to pass from the suddenly-felt dependence to an adult-minded recognition of dependence as a continuing condition of our life. 'Dependence', wrote Dr Harry Guntrip, 'is in fact, an ineradicable element in human nature, and the whole development of love and affection arises out of our needs for one another. From this point of view religion is concerned with the basic fact of personal relationship, and man's quest for a radical solution to the problems that arise out of his dependent nature.' We have in this process to grow into 'the kind of dependence that is an essential part of maturity' and a good deal will depend upon our progress in praying along this road.

We shall have to learn to pass, for example, from the ejaculatory stage – real and important as that is – to the deliberately acknowledged fact of the need for help in the tracts of experience which we learn to scrutinize in quietness. Just as gladness should prompt gratitude, need should evoke confidence. It will not do this unless by our very persistence and importunity we shape our whole attitude to be of the kind that refuses to be put off. It is, of course, reinforced by recognition of the occasions when we have been helped already, and part of the prayer in need can quite usefully pick up recollection of these occasions and use it to reinforce the intensity with which we now pray for help. Importunity does not mean clamour; on the contrary, in all that is suggested here we aim at a deliberate reduction of what is said to the simplest, barest words that can express our approach. There is no need to say more than 'Lord help me', but in the quiet prolongation of this utterance we begin to stretch it over the whole of life to bind ourselves, our need for help and the Lord together in an unbreakable relationship.

To pray in this way for others is an essential part of this relationship and it can be done as simply as we propose to do it for ourselves. In the course of a single day we meet, hear about, receive letters from, remember a great number of people. We can in the moment of remembering them, in the moments after meeting them, pray 'Lord help them', and learn to recall them with greater deliberation at some other time of the day or night. They have needs like our own, peculiar needs of their own, secret needs no other person knows, but the prolonged holding of their needy condition in the attention we give is what really matters. A recognition of their need has been lodged in the fabric of experience.

The moment of exhaustion
The simplest thing to be done at this moment is to 'let go' deliberately. In traditional language it was expressed in words like 'Into thy hands I commend my spirit.' If words like these help

you to pray at such moments use them as fully as you can. If you are not accustomed to them or helped by them, find the shortest phrase that expresses for you the entire act of putting yourself into the keeping of the Other. It may be done with such words as 'I am/We are in your hands', 'We are yours', or simply reflecting 'let go' while you permit your body to relax. It is probable that we should learn to do this regularly and not just leave it to the times of exhaustion, but if we are going to learn to do it at all, we can begin with those desperate moments. What we are doing in this kind of praying is of quite immense importance and is the necessary counterpart to all our striving, all our pleas for help, all our enjoyment, all our conscious addressing of ourselves to the demands of living. 'The night cometh' and it matters a great deal whether its inevitable coming fills us with a sense of panic and emptiness or becomes an occasion for utter relief in letting go ourselves trustfully like a child dropping off to sleep.

But it is not easily learned: all of us carry to the point of exhaustion the accumulations of problems and difficulties. Yet we have argued throughout that praying is a necessary part of truly living, and nowhere is this more true than in respect of the tired, beaten condition which active people find themselves in again and again. To be able to pray 'Let go' is so important a part of our life that it deserves all the practice that it requires to become part of our maturing way of living, and its connection with the final letting go should not be forgotten.

THINKING ABOUT PRAYING

A great many people today ask questions about praying of the kind: 'What are we doing when we pray?' 'What difference does it make?' 'Why do we feel the need for it?' 'Why is it so difficult?' Sooner or later we all encounter some such questions and our practice and thinking about praying are both affected by the questioning. There is a great deal of difference, for example, between the assumption that praying is a kind of withdrawal from the world and a thing that occupies men and women in their solitariness on the one hand, and the assumption that praying is primarily an activity of communion and fellowship,

all-inclusive in its reference, on the other. The position we take
here looks upon prayer as something that issues from and forms
an essential part of this community of all existence. If in the first
part we have dealt with the kind of praying that any of us will
do when we are alone, it should be emphasized now that the
activity of praying nonetheless has its true setting only in the
total life in which we share. We pray for the sake of that total
life; for the sake of its health, for the sake of its purposes, for the
quality of its experiences. We pray that we ourselves and others
may be sensitive to, and in harmony with, its true nature. We
pray that we may be involved fully and rightly with the agoniz-
ing movements of that life as it presses forward to new levels of
achievement.

Holding this belief about the nature of prayer we may
describe it, first of all, as the total response made by the entire
creation to, and in harmony with, the evocative demands of its
maker. It is a saying 'Yes' or 'Amen' to the cosmic purposes. At a
good many levels of being it is possible in a great many ways to
say 'No' – foolish and disastrous as this must ultimately be. If we
say 'No' to the truth of living, we say 'No' to ourselves and begin
to destroy ourselves. This kind of activity could well be called
anti-prayer, and we are all tempted to indulge in it at times and
frequently find ourselves doing it.

Within this total response of saying 'Yes' to God and his purposes, there is the place for our own personal activity and for
that part of it that we are more customarily inclined to call
'praying'. It is with the nature of this special activity that we are
now concerned. Four aspects of it may be considered briefly:

1   *Prayer is a kind of consuming.* Julian Green in his diary wrote
    that such things as spiritual reading which were not consumed
    by prayer and works ended like the Hebrew manna in rotting
    inside us. Charles Péguy wrote that 'a believer is not an ideal-
    ist but a desperately hungry man.' Our praying is akin to a
    deliberate act of chewing over the material of daily experi-
    ence in order that it may become nourishingly part of our-
    selves. The content of the praying is provided by all that we
    see and hear and do and prayer is a process of evaluation.

2 *Prayer is a kind of observing.* It is part of our Christian calling to

> take upon's the mystery of things
> As if we were God's spies,
>
> *King Lear* v.iii.16–17

and to develop the kind of seeing without which we cannot be said to be responsive to God at all. In the practice of prayer focused upon the stuff of everyday experience, we may learn to see particularly and distinctly the nature of things, discriminating and appraising in an ever more and more sensitive fashion. When Péguy in one of his poems put into the mouth of God the observation, 'If there were no Frenchmen, some things I do would never be seen,' he was thus indicating the extreme importance for spiritual growth of this learning to see.

3 *Prayer is a kind of connecting.* The famous line of E. M. Forster's, 'Only connect the prose and the passion and both will be exalted,' is the right kind of pointer here. It is the business of praying to enable us to relate things, to put them in right relationships and right proportions and right perspectives. We are to establish in our prayers links which otherwise would not exist and we are to face and accept those which we might otherwise shun or wish to ignore. We are to grow in a perception of the inter-relatedness of all things; we are to connect our own situation with that of others so that a deep sense of responsibility and communion may be enabled to grow.

4 *Prayer is a kind of resisting.* All living involves a degree of wrestling and there is a point where our involvement in it inevitably brings us to the experience of wrestling Jacob. The kind of resistance with which our praying is concerned includes both the willingness to tackle seemingly intractable experience and the patient maintenance and defence of the positions we have already taken up. Such prayer includes the vigilance and the audacity necessary to keep alive spiritually in circumstances which always threaten to choke and smother us. 'Our fidelities', Péguy wrote, 'are citadels: they do in the long run make, constitute, raise a monument to the face of

God.' Without the prayer of resistance, the best that we already know is likely to be swept away.

These ways of regarding prayer may be described as part of a process of reflection, by which we mean not the kind of reflection which a mirror provides, but that personal activity which takes hold of current experience, sorts it out, faces it, evaluates it and digests it so that it enters fully into the life of action which is our real life. True praying is never divorced from action and could be more properly described as the necessary preparation for the most effective action since that action is most effective which is in line with the purposes of God.

John MacMurray relates it very specifically to action when he writes, 'Religious reflection arises from a failure in personal relationships, and its reference, as a symbolic activity, is to personal relationship: — it is for the sake of active personal relationship — so that the relationship may be resumed in a way that will avoid failure in future.'

Teilhard de Chardin made extensive use of a still more developed sense of reflection, when in *The Phenomenon of Man* he wrote: 'Reflection is the power acquired by a consciousness to turn in upon itself, to take possession of itself as of an object endowed with its own particular consistence and value; no longer merely to know, but to know oneself; no longer merely to know, but to know that one knows.'

Scott Williamson in his book, *Science, Synthesis and Sanity*, approaches this from another angle when he writes of memory: 'In memory the things, situations and events appear as subjective phenomena, for in the translation they have become specifically related to us, thereby acquiring a meaning for ourselves: ... to be alive it is as essential presently to use the medium memory, as it is to use the medium space.'

All these illustrations of how we may regard the practice and nature of praying may help us to see it as something we need to do if as human beings we are to grow up to our full stature. We shall not do this unless we utilize to the full the daily experience we have, and learn to deal with it in a way that is in harmony with the reality in which we are living, i.e. with God. In religious terms this would be called the hallowing or sanctification of things. To attempt to live in any other way is obviously foolish and the outcome of such an attempt is frustration and immaturity. The prayer which we have just described in terms of nourishing, connecting, observing and wrestling is the necessary activity by which experience is mastered, utilized and made coherent so that we grow steadily into the fullness of living.

The setting of all this is the universe itself – God's world – in which his nature initiates, sustains and completes all things. But there can be no doubt that at the present time a great many people find it difficult, if not impossible, to regard the world in this way and a chilling breath of unreality invades their lives for this reason. The things that are most real to them seem to be hemmed in by a meaningless, if not actually hostile, world. Is it possible or worthwhile, they ask, to pray in such a situation? An American literary critic, Hillis Miller, in his book *The Disappearance of God* wrote: 'Post-mediaeval literature records the gradual withdrawal of God from the world. The lines of connection between us and God have broken down. God no longer inheres in a world as the force binding together men and things. There seems to be no way to re-establish the connection.'

Now it should be observed that the connections once regarded as helpful were human constructions and so far they served human beings well. What we are faced with now is the obvious inadequacy of such connections in the setting of a much greater experience of God's world. We need more adequate connections and they will only be apprehended in the processes of praying, in the use of that reflective power we have just mentioned. When Coleridge described the power of imagination as being able to fuse together all the images, thoughts and emotions of the poet's mind, revealing itself 'in the balance and reconciliation of opposite or discordant qualities: of sameness with differences, of the general with the concrete, the idea with the image, the individual with the representative ... a more than usual state of emotion with more than usual order ...' was he not describing what prayer is to do for everyone, difficult and demanding as this must be. The response made by our growing consciousness of God's world is rightly required to pass from less to more adequate levels and it is the business of prayer to reshape the response – to digest the new experience, to observe its qualities, to appreciate its coherence, to resist any falsification of its nature.

Now it may help if we emphasize at this point the counsel which Jesus Christ gave to his friends and reiterated: 'Watch and pray.' Only those who are watching intently are likely, as those words of Péguy reminded us, to see what God is doing and make the consequent connections. What is God doing in his world now? What work is going on in which we are potentially labourers? What agony is being endured before which we are counselled to keep awake? Inseparable from praying, this watching must form an essential part of our growth in spirituality. If, going through the vale of misery, we have no eyes to see the wells on whose resources to draw, we are defeated already. If, confronted with the handiwork of God in new shapes we take fright and turn back, how shall we ever learn to grow?

It is in the immediate context of daily life that most of us are called on to develop this watchfulness, and in praying to make our own the truth which the experience affords. This is what Jesus Christ discovered and lived by, being wholly open to and responsive to the truth revealed in every situation. We, up to the limits of our capacity, are likewise set to learn that way of living, and in virtue of our daily encounter with, and participation in, such things as family life and marriage, work and play, health and sickness, are to make our own what all these things can yield. Some things will come to us with a blinding flash of illumination, others will be wrung out from lengthy experience by patient long-suffering. Praying is the activity that covers both these kinds of experience and relates them, for we need both and we need to be able to connect them. When in Shakespeare's *Tempest*, Ferdinand first sees Miranda, there bursts from his whole being the cry 'Oh, you wonder!' and our praying should have some of that utterly delighted perception in it. But the whole of life is not contained in the experience of falling in love at first sight. 'Ripeness is all,' and there must be a kind of praying which springs from the mature knowledge of the costly character of the love that endures.

In the face of such experience as daily life provides we are

called upon to make a great many decisions, and their quality
will depend to a great extent upon the 'ordering' of our attitude
effected through praying. Either we respond with 'off the cuff'
decisions, prompted by fears, jealousies, fads, enthusiasms, or we
respond out of imaginative, sensitive, integrated many-sided
awareness of the time, event and question. Prayer that has built
up a coherent generously-conceived structure for living is clearly
involved in all such moments, and not least when we make some
bad decisions and see others as mediocre and feeble.

For praying must provide bases, motives and resources for
recovery and renewal. It must use those frames of reference provided already by the Church in Scriptures and Sacraments and
accustom us to review what we have done in relation to them
and to the demands of everyday living. What we need in this
respect is the kind of praying that can generate the conviction
that at forty, fifty or sixty years it is possible and worthwhile to
begin again when some devastating experience has shown how
frail and insecure has been the structural ordering so far. Since
it is likely that such experiences will be felt more keenly the
longer we have tried to go this way, and the degree to which they
are felt is a measure of actual growth, we need still greater help
as we go on. The more we become acquainted with evil and
good, the more sensitive we are to joy or despair, the more the
importance of such praying is confirmed. Unless, indeed, we are
learning to pray in this fashion, failures and temptations corrupt,
turning people into hypocrites and churches into devils' covens.

Finally we must recognize that prayer must provide for steps
of advance, foreseeing, visualizing, prompting new ventures
and grasping the significance of decisions which shape the
future. Prayer extrapolates our vision. Teilhard de Chardin
wrote: 'Each one of us has his Jacob's ladder, whose rungs are
formed of a series of objects,' and the job of praying is to discern and lay hold of the objects which are possible ladder-
rungs; otherwise we remain in an arrested, immobile condition,
unwilling to leave what has so far been attained, doubtful and
fearful about the future. It is the task of the church community
in its encouragement of all its members to pray to keep before
them the biblical sense of a never-ending journey and to

provide the necessary 'communion' which at each stage
empowers us and heartens us to go on. 'Little by little, we may
rest assured, the work is being done ... one day the whole
divinizible substance of matter will have passed into the souls
of men' and we shall be enriched by all that God has created.
Prayer, in the meanwhile, is the activity by which we select,
appraise and utilize what we can as we go along.

'Prayer could be silent, a way of being in the world, an inward
and outward bearing, a constant striving for increased awareness
of the world, and for the active love, ever renewed, which must
accompany this striving.' These words occur in Dumitriu's novel
Incognito, and they sum up much that has been said earlier. This
'way of being in the world' is what matters and it clearly involves
all that a man or woman is or hopes to be. We are what we pray.

7

PRAYER IN TIME OF
STRESS AND CRISIS

It has often been said that many of us only turn to prayer when things go badly wrong, when all other means of remedying or dealing with a situation have ben exhausted. Nothing else is now left that we can do, so we must turn to prayer. You see it in Shakespeare's play *The Tempest* when the mariners cry in the midsts of the storm at sea, 'All lost! To prayers, to prayers! all lost!' There is, of course, just enough truth in this observation to make us wince, to remind us that a good deal of our praying is indeed at the mercy of circumstances.

> The devil was sick, the devil a monk would be,
> The devil was well, the devil a monk was he!

We can be bad-weather as well as fair-weather Christians.

Admitting all this, there still remains the question of how to pray when evil things and cruel circumstances are upon us, when we have done all that lies in our power to do and face the horror that remains. How are we to pray in such desperate times?

> For innumerable troubles are come about me:
> my sins have taken such hold upon me
>   that I am not able to look up:
> yea, they are more in number than the hairs of
>   my head,
> and my heart hath failed me.

> Psalm 40.12

Let's pause for a moment over the word 'desperate'. It is used fairly often to describe moments of crisis and times of great strain. It has been said that birth is a desperate business and rebirth even more so. But 'desperate' has to do with despair, with the loss of all hope, with a final surrender, and we should not get into the habit of using it too often to mean even the most terrible anguish. It may well be that some praying will have to stand between us and such final despair, and while we can still pray we still have hope. Some praying may have to take the form of saying 'No' to despair. One of the most moving poems, called 'Carrion Comfort', by the poet Gerard Manley Hopkins, was devoted to just that theme. Don't let's belittle such a prayer.

But what are we to do as the dreadful situation, whatever it is, closes in on us? Hopelessness grows more terrible as men and women come to think there is no one, human or divine, to whom they can turn. To be alone is the last stage of their misery, and this is so because to be human is to be a creature who from birth onwards turns to someone else, to parents, friends, lovers and God, to be confirmed in our very being. If they looked through us as if we were not there, we should die in despair. We turn to them because they give a meaning to our lives. It may not be a pleasant or happy meaning, it may be hard to say exactly what meaning it is, but we turn to them expecting that kind of assurance. We must be assured that we are not alone.

Nonetheless, we come to times when this 'aloneness' is forced upon us, when we do not know where to turn for reassurance. All this is set before us in its extremest form in the description of Christ's agony in the Garden of Gethsemane. It gives us our best clue to praying in such times, for it leaves no doubt in our minds that he was at that time beset by the most terrible agony of mind and spirit which racked his body too. We can believe that it was centred upon not his own fate in execution by the Romans but upon the truth or otherwise of the way he had set before men and women. Had he devoted his life to a monstrous delusion?

Now this praying has one supreme concern. It is to put himself into the Father's hands, to put all that his life's work amounted to into those hands, to assert that all things are in such hands. This is why I think that all our attempts to pray are important, however childish they may be, however marred by our fears or plain selfishness, because they can help to build up a bit more of that sense of 'THOU art there'. All the long history of Christ's people turns upon that assertion, that act of faith, that final declaration. We are to learn to pray through all our years, through good times and bad, so that our rebirth, painful and full of anguish, may not be without hope. 'If I go down to hell, thou art there also' (Psalm 139.7). He descended into hell certainly, but we may pray, even in the approaches to it, 'Thou art there also.' 'We are in your hands.' Perhaps we can say no more than this, but this is all that finally matters.

8

PRAYER AS A PROBLEM OF TRANSPORT

For every man hath business and desire,
Such as it is, – and for mine own poor part,
I'll go pray.

Hamlet i.v.130–2

How to 'go pray' is, for most of us, one of the most difficult things in living. It is easier to turn away from it and to try to dodge the difficulty, but from time to time, 'just when we're safest', some mine is sprung beneath our feet and we are nagged again by this insistent need to pray. It may be hard to define; it may be 'somewhere in the room' like Mrs Gradgrind's pain, but we cannot escape from it. Questions are constantly being asked about it wherever people turn to consider what living entails. Churchgoing may be at a very low ebb but the interest in praying goes on. Like Paul Dombey interrogating his father about money, people ask us directly to tell them, not only what prayer is, but to tell them 'what can it do'. Being warned by that Dickensian incident we may forbear to answer that 'it can do everything', and set ourselves in humbler fashion to try to answer out of our own experience what we understand by praying and what we believe it does.

This is not an occasion for producing examples of 'answers to prayer.' One good thing about living in the age of lotteries and premium-bonds is that we must needs meet a degree of sophistication about that kind of answer. If we are going to help at all we have got to begin somewhere outside that unconvincing territory that is so often regarded as the average churchgoer's experience of prayer. The assumptions made about this may often be quite unfair but we have got to recognize their presence.

75

People in exile are not helped by being told how their problems can be solved in the land they have left, and most of us are in exile today. Sooner or later most of us are going to find things we trusted in taken from us. How do you sing the Lord's song in a strange land?

We have been given 'an hearty desire to pray'. Is this really true? Is it possible to begin our exploration of our human condition with this in mind? Are we ready to suspend our disbelief long enough to follow the line wherever it leads, as Paul Klee invites us to do in his pictures? Without minimizing the difficulties, this attempt of mine does start from the conviction that to be human is to be overtaken by a desire to pray. It belongs, like a great number of not-easily-sorted-out impulses to the human condition, making itself felt in quite unpredictable ways, coming and going without any very clear reference to other aspects of our experience.

It found an extensive expression in *The Prelude* in which Wordsworth frequently uses words like 'yearnings', 'misgivings', and 'undetermined' about experiences which plainly meant much to him. He knew that they awed, consoled, agitated, quietened, troubled, and shaped his being. He believed that an openness to such promptings was of immense importance in the spiritual growth of human beings. He was equally ready to admit the fugitive uncontrollable character of these responses.

It is possible to adopt a disparaging attitude to all such intimations, to be scornful about this kind of romantic experience, to opt for 'the dry hardness' which a critic like T. E. Hulme demanded for literature in our time, to argue that the light that never was on land or sea had the effect of drug-taking and left men and women ill-prepared to face the light of ordinary day. But we can sympathize with an aversion to romanticism without accepting the insistence on confining ourselves to those things that are bounded by a firm hard line, without foregoing our recognition of those things which obstinately refuse to be so bounded. Things we feel sure about do not of necessity have outlines of this kind. They do not lack reality even if we are unable to contain them in our words of measurements. 'Human will, human understanding,' wrote Buber, 'are not everything.

There is some reality confronting us. We cannot forget it for a moment.... I come at a certain moment to a wall, to a boundary, to a limit that I cannot ignore.'

What we need at that point is not definition but the kind of imaginative apprehension which Coleridge spoke of, an imagination which proved to be a more, not less, orderly coherence-seeking activity than prosaic observation. It not only enabled men and women to see more in their experience, but it also enabled them to 'connect more', to relate more, to unify more. Not all people possess such imagination, not all who have known it possess it all the time. But we can learn to come awake with the assistance of those whose spirits are already awakened. We can learn to be expectant by paying attention to those who already see and are able to tell us what they see. So we may hope to grow into that human condition which will be found responsive sometime and to some degree to the music that creeps by us on the waters, and praying is one of the channels of response.

Why then should Hamlet betake himself to prayer? Suppose that we substituted for the Shakespearean version a more commonplace demand that he 'must think this out'. Clearly he needed time to face the problems of his relations with the ghost, his uncle, his mother, Ophelia, Rosencrantz and Guilderstern, and with himself. Does the introduction of the word 'pray' add anything of importance or change the mode of address towards his problems? Would it help those who are inquiring about the nature of prayer if we asked them to consider what difference they thought obtained between setting themselves to look critically, courageously, good-humouredly, sanely, and imaginatively at some issues and praying about them?

Here again I want to plead hurriedly for a withholding at this point of what is so often treated as the trump card – the introduction of the name of God – not because I do not see it all related to God, but because I do not believe that it is going at this moment to be helpful to the people I have in mind. Shouting our convictions at other people is not much help anyway. Nothing is gained by giving the impression that all the problems of praying are resolved if only you believe in God. Those who do some praying know that that is not so, and some of them may well say that they learned something about believing in God because they prayed and not the other way around. The Shakespearean Hamlet no doubt had his own sense of how God came into all this, and it would be a fascinating problem to explore the suggestions given in the play as to what this amounted to: but we cannot invoke that for ourselves and our own needs. For a great many people God-believed-in is not in the picture as yet, and I go all the way with them in being reluctant to look for God who will answer the bell.

This is not to be precious about God so that we cannot admit him into the menial conditions of living. The Christ has already made it abundantly clear that he is ready to do and does do whatever menial task is needed to be done. But this is endeavouring to steer clear of pressing the bell like irresponsible children to see if he will answer it. It is trying to keep as close as possible to the question of what praying is for one perplexed in the extreme like Hamlet or Othello.

Some years ago, in an essay entitled *Distance and Relation*, Martin Buber described his view of the nature of humanity, and distinguished two aspects of the way in which men and women dealt with their experience, which is where we see what being a human being is like. He called them 'Setting at a distance' and 'Drawing into relation', and this distinction enabled him to go further and to emphasize the importance of the Between. Indeed everything that mattered turned upon the nature of what lay between men and women and between human beings and God. You could have almost anything – from the equivalent of high tariff walls designed to protect home industry to the Shekinah of God. The self-made man like Mr Bounderby in *Hard Times* clearly did not want either God or man to look over his walls, and he is as good a picture as we can find of the person for whom the Between has shrunk to near-vanishing point. He just could not set at a distance nor draw into relation any human being because he could not concede that degree of freedom to them. Buber, it should be noticed, saw the distance set between the Ark of God and the people as they journeyed as a symbol of the importance of the Between. There was a space affording scope and room for the growth of awe, trust, affection,

recognition, dialogue and wonder. Sensitiveness to others, to the
Other, does not stand much chance of genuine growth if we are
not able to stand at such a distance from them as enables us to
appreciate the true proportions, lineaments and features of the
thing or person we contemplate.

> Great things are done when men and mountains meet.
> They are not done by jostling in the street.

What Blake points to is the distancing which mountains confront us with before there can be any question of drawing into
relation. The sense of wonder and awe in relation to the other
needs not only to be sparked off, but needs also to be saved from
being displaced by artificial substitute versions which men and
women have been only too ready to exploit both in social life
and religion. We need, again and again, to be jolted out of our
assumptions about the nature of things, and to be compelled to
see them in terms 'passing strange'.

Such an office is done for us by an artist who has himself seen
the particularity of some things which we have come to take for
granted and are therefore failing to see at all. The Scriptures
have a good deal to say about this business of seeing and not
seeing. We can almost hear the opponents of Jesus Christ
exclaiming with Hamlet's mother: 'Why seems it so particular
with thee?' The battle over sight and insight goes on all the time,
and if we prove to be too indolent of heart to perceive what the
prophets and artists are showing us, we may have to learn by a
yet harder way – as Joseph did in the pit into which his brothers
had cast him.

One way or another our soul's health depends upon this distancing. The means an artist employs to bring about the sharp
separation and the new relation constitute his artistic capability.
Vincent van Gogh, who reflected a good deal upon this matter,
said that he wanted to put the radiance to human beings that
was once expressed by giving them haloes, but which he believed
could be done in other ways today. Martin Buber extends the
insight: 'Consider great nude sculptures of the ages. None of
them is to be understood properly either from the givenness of
the human body or from the will to expression of an inner state,

but solely from the relational event which takes place between the two entities which have gone apart from one another, the withdrawn "body" and the withdrawing "soul".'

The various forms employed in the different arts represent new attempts to set at a distance and to draw to relations, whether the concern is with the human body of the natural world or perceptions of human experience. Santayana, in his novel *The Last Puritan*, relates it finally to our concern for praying: 'Singing isn't talking or doing business. It is more like praying, or as you say, like letting out the inner man that circumstances have suppressed.'

But few of us are artists. What entry into the sphere of the Between, what setting at a distance and drawing into relation, are we to make? The answer is that we are to pray, and that praying, faint and immature as it may be, is our 'venture into the interior'. Its true character is exploratory. It is to enable us to go beyond ourselves, to make the acquaintance of the Other in the only conditions in which this can be done.

It is not absurd to describe it as a matter of transport though it has been also spoken about in terms of putting off your shoes. You step out of the familiar, you are caught up, you go into a desert, you go into an inner room and shut the door, you are carried away by a blinding glimpse; all of these are saying that we have to be transported. It is not difficult to see why comparisons are made with the 'trips' of the drug addict, and why there are similarities in the descriptions of the heightened states of consciousness in prayer and drug-taking. We are not likely to be helpful if we too summarily dismiss the awkward questions which arise when our 'transports of delight' are being scrutinized. The Apostles at Pentecost must have found it difficult to persuade their critics that they were intoxicated by God and not by alcohol. The Dionysiac element has hovered on the confines of many religions and how to baptize it is a continuing problem. It is not likely to go away if we try to ignore it. Santayana's Puritan found himself wondering, 'Was it right to be transported out of oneself at all? Wasn't it just shirking, a mere escape and delusion? Wasn't it what had created all false religions?' To reply that it can be but need not necessarily be so is to be required to state clearly what form of transport we are choosing and why. If we choose to accompany Hamlet in praying we must try to make clear our reasons for so doing.

The answer which is attempted here springs from what has already been described as a kind of nagging that goes on, as if reminding us that there is something rooted in us that will not be silenced. That it can be finally put out of action I do not doubt. Suicide in one way or another is always an option. To say that ceasing to pray is a form of suicide sounds outrageous even though we sing it in one of our Lenten hymns. I prefer to go back to the nagging experience and to ask what this really means. I am not thinking of it as the cry of conscience that tells me that I ought to pray but as the voice of something in me which says I want to pray, only it doesn't use those words. To understand it at all I have to go backward and take a new look at the kind of transport into the Beyond which I and others have known already, which we all knew when we began to play.

Most of us are aware of the revolution which has taken place in the field of education since we have learned to recognize the importance of play. We have lived long enough to have seen the M'Choakumchilds put to flight from our schools. We are not quite so familiar with the lines of thought set out by Hugo Rahner in *Man at Play*, by Huizinga in *Homo Ludens*, and by Harvey Cox in *The Feast of Fools*, nor have we found clear ways of relating what they say to us to the life of men and women in the Church. Perhaps this is why so much of our praying remains a kind of nagging duty instead of being a joy. This thinking that brings playing and praying together may well be the help we needed to illuminate the subject, and if we are going to make the best use of it we may find the opening for it in the reconsideration of art itself.

To return to Hamlet, we can say that what he needed was not so much the opportunity to think out his situation but the chance to play it out, and that that, in all sorts of ways, was what he managed to do. 'The play's the thing,' not just to catch the conscience of a king, but to enable him to perceive more clearly what he was faced by and to enter more understandingly into that situation. From the moment he began to pray about it

Hamlet became the fantastic player whom it became easy to call
mad. Do not believe it: he is never more sane than when he is
playing. His tragedy is nowhere more painfully expressed than in
meeting death as he plays the foils with Laertes.

Does this mean that playing is futile? Not in the least.
Neither praying nor playing are insurances against tragedy, nor
can they resist Death's strict arrest. There is One who played
out his play riding in triumph into the city where men were
determined to kill him, breaking bread with friends who were to
desert him, standing his trial before administrators of law
whose perplexities made it a grim farce. It would be childish
indeed to suppose that playing and praying are magical wea-
pons to defeat the evil in the world. We are concerned with
something quite different: the childlike ability to transcend these
things by including them in the scope of praying and playing.
And we who watch that play

> See at his feet
> Some fragment from his dream of human life,
> Shaped by himself,

and we know that the play is not over, but rather calls for new
actors who no doubt will make just such a botched affair of it as
Bottom and his friends did, but do it with the nearest they can
get to pure love, and that suffices.

Yet we have some difficulty in seeing our praying in this company. Harvey Cox insists that we should be less concerned to
wring our hands about the apparent neglect of what has traditionally been regarded as praying, and be more ready to see a
much wider connotation given to it and quicker to see widespread evidence of its practice. 'Anyone who gives vent to joy,
sorrow or gratitude, or refuses to be bound by the narrow world
of fact is really living a prayer.' The Hamlet who

> ... could be bounded in a nutshell,
> And count myself a king of infinite space,
>
> *Hamlet* II.ii.264

is the praying and playing Hamlet.

All this must be related to the interaction of parts which

constitutes liturgical corporate prayer, for it is here that we encounter the evidences of impoverishment writ large. 'There was never a merry world', wrote Selden, 'since the fairies stopped dancing and the parson stopped conjuring.' Liturgical reform will have to become a great deal more foolish and playful if it is ever to catch not merely the conscience but also the heart and soul of humanity. Drop-out movements which so frequently manifest interest in forms of meditation and forms of communion should not go unnoticed. They are in part at least a hopeful radical affirmation, 'not an escape from the world but the first step in its recreation.' What we must look for on the whole front of creative artistry are the things that can stab us awake, help us to see connections, help us to see the unaccountable figures in the furnace. Better that imagination should run riot than it should be starved. Biblical imagery is there, not to do duty for all time, but to make clear to successive generations that they too must play with the sublime, they too must entertain strangers with imaginative generosity.

All this can make no headway till more men and women are willing to make their own forms of intercession, thanksgiving, and penitence more clearly playful in the sense of loosening the imagination, and showing others what it amounts to. This is not a plea for elaborate designs. The child who plays with absorption with a couple of pegs and a tin can is the model. But the adult version of it has got to be humble enough to admit that it needs the help of the artist and player. It has to learn and re-learn what aspiration, what gratitude, what compassion mean and look like in the 'house not built with hands'. It means that we take a new look at our intercession leaflets and our aids to prayer, and inquire about their likelihood of sparking off the spirit.

> PRINCE HAL Do thou stand for my father and examine me upon the particulars of my life.
>
> FALSTAFF Shall I? Content. This chair shall be my state, this dagger my sceptre and this cushion my crown.
>
> *1 Henry IV* II.iv.358–61

Of course it is excellent fooling, but have we grasped what it means to be made fools for Christ's sake? Or a spectacle to the world? Or a laughing-stock? 'We artists', wrote Durrell, 'form one of those pathetic human chains which human beings form to pass buckets of water up to a fire, or to bring in a lifeboat. An uninterrupted chain of humans born to explore the inward riches of the solitary life on behalf of the unheeding unforgiving community, manacled together by the same gift.' Not only to put out fires but to give living water, not only to rescue from drowning but to launch out into the deep: these too are the functions of this artistry that plays and prays with singleness of mind. As Christians addressed to our common task in this same chain-like relation we are bidden to sing, for it is by continuing to do so that we retain our humanity on which the grace of God is to work. To be thus transported is to play as the prophet saw children playing in the streets of the Holy City, and to pray as we are bidden.

9

THE PARISH MEETING
AT WORK

INTRODUCTION

This is not an attempt to discuss the significance of the Parish Meeting and its place in the life of the Church today. It is simply concerned with practical matters arising out of the work of the Meeting. Almost every week, inquiries are made about the conduct of the Meeting – 'How do you begin? What do you do? What are the difficulties?' – and it is to try to answer these questions that these notes have been put together. There are no authorities on the Parish Meeting; there are only those who are working away in their parishes and finding out for themselves what tremendous things are happening. Nevertheless there is now a body of experience to draw upon for help and guidance for those who are just beginning. Some use of this experience may help to sustain newcomers in their times of difficulty.

As practical advice, it nevertheless raises the most far-reaching questions, and it has been necessary to say a little about the way in which we regard the Parish Meeting. We misconceive the matter if we suppose that it does not raise questions which affect our whole conception of the life of the Church, the work of the clergy, and the position of the laity. It asks indeed that we should re-examine the whole job of the Church in the context of our changing world. No one is more affected by this than the parish priest. Most thoughtful men are conscious of this, of the need to revise their conception of the work of the ministry, of the extent to which the field of parochial work has altered.

The Parish Meeting has come into being as a reflection of this change. Emphatically it is not a way of escape from difficulties nor an easy attempt to find a solution. Throughout these notes, the work of the parish priest is described in terms that call for more, not less, imagination, faith, and courage. Indeed it may well appear that the capacity of the parish priest to adapt himself to the changed relationships that the Meeting calls for and that the times suggest, is *the* fundamental problem. From time to time we hear of Parish Meetings being dropped – 'because they did not work'. Behind that explanation is most commonly to be found an incomplete understanding of what is really needed, and as a consequence, an attempt to carry on the Meeting in ways which were self-defeating. It is true to say that no one has more to learn from the Parish Meeting than the parish priest himself. He can learn more from it than from almost anything else. The root question is whether we really want to learn. To those who do, these comments on the day-to-day problems of the Parish Meeting are addressed.

WHAT IT IS AND HOW TO BEGIN

The Parish Meeting is the assembling of the local church, the church in the parish, in order that it may realize and work out its essential life. It is a meeting whose character is implied in the New Testament word 'fellowship'. It is a meeting, the agenda or business of which is the whole life and work of the Christian Community in the world. It can be described on the one hand with the utmost simplicity: that week by week the members of the church in the parish meet together to talk over, plan, execute, and report upon the work of the Christian Church in whose life they share. It must be recognized on the other hand that in this matter we are making the most tremendous claims: that this meeting is nothing less than the representation of the Body of Christ, which in the very power and commission of Pentecost is setting about its work and revealing its life. We are not talking about an organization devised by a parish priest and enjoyed by some parishioners. We are not talking about a study group, a prayer meeting, a business meeting, a consultative committee, a social. We are not thinking in terms of Chairman, Secretary, minutes, correspondence, and agenda. We are talking about the Church, whose primary business is to be the Church. The Parish

Meeting is to be thought of in these overwhelming terms or it is better left alone.

How then do we arrive at this? In every parish church, Sunday by Sunday, a number of Christian people come together to take part in an act of worship. When this is concluded, they disperse. They have 'been to church'. Very many of them do not meet or see each other again until they repeat this 'going to church'. Some of them belong to and take part in various social functions arranged by various organizations, for boys and girls, men and women. From each of these things they derive much that is important, delightful, and valuable.

A few people, however, have possibly felt that there is something missing from this weekly round as the expression of the corporate life of the Christian Church. The services may well have been offered to God with all sincerity and earnestness, with beauty and devotion; the social and moral witness afforded by one or more of the organizations may have been diligently and courageously performed. But is this the whole of Christian life? Is this all that the membership of Christ's Body means? Is there not something else, presupposed alike by the services and the personal witness, something else out of which the services and the personal witness may be said to issue, which is unfortunately scarcely visible and hardly known, to which could be given a name like 'the Body' or 'the Fellowship'? Is there not something else, more conscious of itself and its work than the congregation in the pews can often claim to be, more active, disciplined, purposeful, informed, and spiritually alert than the meetings of the organizations that we know?

The parish priest knows only too well that he finds himself praying, 'Would that there were', for apart from this even the most successful organizations and the most uplifting services would appear to be almost beside the point. For the services are the services of the Church, and the organizations are designed to be the handmaids and servants of the Church. But what is the Church? What is its shape, its look, its nature, and its purpose?

Once in a year, the people of the parish are still summoned to a meeting of the Church: the Annual Parochial Church Meeting. A comprehensive agenda is provided, which by the inclusion of 'other matters of parochial and general Church interest', is made as wide as anyone could wish it to be. In practice the financial, electoral, and domestic issues of the life of the congregation occupy most of the time, so that little opportunity is afforded to anyone to be able to see how the business transacted springs from or is related to the doctrines, devotion, and witness of the Christian Church. How rarely do we pause in the conduct of this annual meeting to give ourselves liberty to examine the Christian significance of what we are doing! 'But there isn't time, this is not the place.' Exactly. Where then is the place and when is the time, for the Christian congregation to be able to examine its corporate life and purpose? Such examination is plainly necessary for many reasons. The general confessions of the Church services certainly imply general self-examinations; if not, they are reduced to being simultaneous personal confessions. The evangelistic work of the Church is certainly supposed to be more than the efforts of the incumbent. The pastoral concern of the Church does not exempt its individual members from a particular responsibility in these matters. But where, when, and how are all these things to become the genuine concern of the members of the Church if we have only the Annual Meeting?

It is when we are ready to see what is involved in this demand that we can recognize how right and necessary the Parish Meeting is. We can explain for the moment that such a meeting is the Annual Meeting shorn of its lone dignity, and freed from the constraints of endeavouring to work through an agenda for which so little time is allowed that it inevitably becomes almost entirely lacking in Christian significance. Let us suppose that we convert our annual meeting into a weekly meeting or add to our annual meeting fifty-one other opportunities to grapple with 'other matters of parochial and general Church interest'. We have, by so doing, given the members of the Church the opportunity and the responsibility of doing so much more than the Annual Meeting could ever hope to do. We have provided ourselves with the opportunity for all those matters, evangelistic, pastoral, devotional, which it is properly the concern of the members of the Church to face and consider. But we have done more than this. We have given the opportunity for the Church to assemble to be the Church, and we can begin to discover what it really looks like and what its work is.

How then do we begin? Almost everything depends upon the right approach which so far we have implied in theological terms. To this conception of the Parish Meeting as the assembling of the Church we must constantly return if we are to deal wisely with the problems that arise. It should be emphasized from the beginning that in holding the Parish Meeting we are not creating another organization in the parish to which people who have a taste for discussion or an evening to spare can come. Indeed, we cannot hope to find a place in the crowded week of so many parochial organizations for the Parish Meeting unless we can lift it right out of the sphere of competition from the outset. In the long run we shall not be able to sustain it in the face of difficulties unless we can regard it as of obligation.

All this means that in practice we must begin at a point beyond the usual idea of a discussion group or Padre's hour. It means also that we must begin at a point beyond the Parochial Church Councils. We shall discuss in greater detail later on the relationship between the Parish Meeting and the Parochial Church Council. Here it may be said that we are concerned with something older than the statutory organizations; and to the churchwarden who once objected that he did not find Parish Meetings in the Enabling Act, we should reply that even so we find them in the New Testament.

It is important, therefore, that before the Parish Meeting is begun some members of the congregation should understand this very well and should be willing to accompany the parish priest when he sets out on this adventurous course. It should be explained as carefully as possible from the pulpit or discussed more fully in a parochial Convention before the first meeting is held. No doubt should be left in the minds of the members of the congregation that while we are not investing our own creation with sacred authority, we are endeavouring to allow the embodiment of something which is holy, which is Christ's, and which is our most sacred concern.

This means in practice that we must choose one night of the

week for the Meeting, and see that no organization holds its meetings at this time. We should not dream of allowing such a thing to occur at the time when the whole family of the Church was met together for the Holy Communion. We must be no less exacting for the Parish Meeting. It is worthwhile spending some time in both clearing the ground for the Parish Meeting in the weekly parochial time-table and in making it clear that it will be a fixture when it is established.

Is it necessary to meet weekly? Quite obviously local circumstances must be considered, but it is our conception of the nature of the meeting that must determine our decision. We usually expect that the congregation of the faithful will assemble each week for worship. This meeting is the counterpart, the other self, of the worshipping body. The occasions of its meeting should certainly be not less frequent than the minimum attendance which we look for in the life of the worshipping Church.

Whom shall we expect to come? It is clear that we shall look for the assembling of all those who take seriously their membership of Christ's Church. It is right that they should be asked to attend. As soon as the newly-confirmed have taken their place in the communicating at the altar, it is right to expect and invite them to be present at this meeting. Young and old, girls and boys, men and women, all are there, because of our common life in the Body of Christ.

No doubt the practical difficulties appear to be immense. 'How is it possible', asks someone, 'to expect such varieties of ages to be at ease and at home in one meeting?' 'How is it possible', asks another, 'to keep the interest sustained for such diverse groups? 'How is it possible', asks a third, 'if the worshipping congregation already numbers several hundreds?'

For most of these and many kindred questions there are now some answers provided by experience, and further experience will certainly enable us to extend them. Quite clearly it can never be easy to sustain the interest of the younger people on some aspects of the business of the Meeting, and it is equally true that most adults find it no less difficult at times. What matters is our use of common sense about this, and particularly in the case of the parish priest when he is actually guiding the progress of the Meeting. It is a matter of experience that it is wiser to be ready to deal with most subjects in instalments carried over several weeks than to try to cover them in a single meeting.

The agenda of every meeting should normally contain a variety of subjects, touching all kinds of aspects of the Christian life, and the one who steers the Meeting should be alert enough to recognize when it is time to leave one subject for another. That does not mean that big demands on the attention should not be made, but it does mean that the leader should be intensely aware of the difference between hard-working and over-working. In an age which frequently laments the lost art of conversation, it is not likely that we shall become masters of group discussion in a few weeks. Inevitably we shall make mistakes, and people will be bewildered, confused, over-talkative, far too glib, over-reticent, resentful, suspicious. Inevitably we shall lose some people after experiences of this kind. Those who tend to monopolize the conversation will have their victims, and those who look for neat and tidy results will complain that we seem to talk and get nowhere. It is then that we shall need to be reminded that we go into this business of the Parish Meeting as a matter of obligation, determined to carry it through when it no longer proves to be so exciting.

The question of numbers is also a matter in which experience alone can help us. In practice the number of people who will put themselves to the trouble of attending a weekly meeting of this kind is far smaller than the number of those who will 'go to church' for services. We are much more likely in most parishes to be concerned with tens than with hundreds. Even so, the best possible way of enabling hundreds of fellow Christians to work out the implications of their common Christian life can be discovered only by practice. Such experience as we have already suggests certainly that there is a limit to the number of people who can enter into this entirely informal and very personal relationship of the Parish Meeting, and that, where numbers continued to grow, a hiving-off process might conceivably be the solution. But so far we are not faced with this kind of difficulty.

What we have to face at the moment is the great problem of how to use every moment of the Meeting so as to enable the very mixed group of people who attend to take the fullest part in what is going on. To deal with those problems we shall need to discuss the actual running of the Meeting.

One further point, however, may be dealt with here. It has been objected from time to time that the title 'Parish Meeting' is a misnomer, since only a very small proportion of the people in the parish attends. To this we may reply at once that the same objection may be levelled at the 'Parish Communion', and, today, with some justice at the Book of Common Prayer. Our use of this title is more a declaration of our purpose than of our achievement. We are trying to make it clear that this meeting is for everyone and not for a few. We are trying to throw down from our side any barriers that might otherwise be thought to exist. At all costs we must resist the tendency to assemble a small coterie or clique. We must do everything we can to make it clear that the Meeting welcomes all who are willing to come. Names which suggest any narrower basis are therefore to be avoided. There is nothing final in the use of 'Parish Meeting'. If someone can think of a better name, by all means let us use it. In the country districts, especially, there may be some confusion with the civic Parish Meeting. What matters is the making clear that while we use the Parish as our territorial basis and as an indication of our sphere of action, our doors are open to all. Our picture of the Meeting is that of people in a series of concentric rings according to the degree with which they see their attachment and obligation to the Body. They are moving backwards and forwards continually, pressing more closely to the heart of it when spirits are kindled, retreating in times of coldness and disillusionment. This continual shift and change in attachment and response is part of life. What still matters is our sense of belonging to the Body and our admitted need to come back to it.

THE CONDUCT OF THE MEETING

Where shall we hold the Meeting? The question is not unimportant, because our intention is to try to get as far as we can from the usual atmosphere of meetings. We are thinking in terms of a family coming together and it is in the setting of a home that we should most naturally desire to meet. How can we get this? It is far better to be crowded in the Vicarage than to be spaciously accommodated in the Parish Hall or the School. That does not mean that we must rule out either of these, but that we must always take trouble to see that the impression given by the surroundings is friendly, informal, unofficial, and capable of making people feel at ease with each other.

The force of this applies specially to the actual conduct of the Meeting. What is the job of the parish priest in this respect? From the beginning it should be understood that his position here is vastly different from that of the preacher in the pulpit, the chairman in the chair, the lecturer on the platform, simply because the Meeting itself is different from any other kind of gathering. The people here are not assembled to hear an address but to talk together, to communicate with each other, and therefore the chief thing is to enable that activity to become as valuable as we can make it. On the other hand the conversation is not aimless and it requires steering. The parish priest is possibly the best person for the job, but this should not be taken for granted, and it is important that the Meeting should not become totally dependent upon his being there. While the very nature of the Meeting as we have described it makes it clear that normally he will be there, the Meeting must certainly go on when he is absent. It must be possible to call on others to take his place as a result of the experience they have gained from being familiar with the way in which it is done. Nor should it be taken for granted that the parish priest knows immediately how to perform this difficult task. He is there in the position of a learner like everyone else, and is just as likely to make mistakes. Indeed, a good deal of his background and training makes the position particularly difficult for him, accustomed as he is to preaching – the very last thing that is needed at the Meeting.

The steering of the Meeting is, even so, a different matter from the art of competent chairmanship, because the people have not come together primarily to transact business. They are gathered together as fellow-Christians, and the primary job of the Meeting is two-fold like this title. It must bring out as clearly as possible what being 'fellows' means and what this relationship implies. In this sense, the job of the Meeting is to enable Christians to discover something more of the truth about themselves, to find a more real meaning and a deeper content in the phrases that they have heard so often. That is why each Meeting, however confused it may become, has something Pentecostal about it. The biblical foundation should never be forgotten. 'Then they that feared the Lord spake often one to another, and the Lord hearkened and heard it.'

There can be no question then of allowing a contemptuous dismissal of the Meeting as 'just talk', because it does not set out to follow the usual lines of a business meeting, or to carry decisions by votes, or to draw up its conclusions in a series of neat 'findings'. There may be something much more honest and edifying in arriving at a confession of ignorance, bafflement, and something like humiliation, felt by all those present, and not least by the parish priest himself. Put very simply, his job is to get people to talk, to overcome those barriers of shyness and reserve, to be natural and honest and unaffected with each other. In talking of almost anything connected with religion this is far more difficult for most people than it sounds. Here apparently more than anywhere else we are determined to 'keep up appearances' and to talk vaguely and as generally as possible lest we should give ourselves away. The fact that someone with a good deal of courage shows us how it can be done and bravely goes ahead in an honest declaration does not by any means win the unqualified approval of others. It has indeed been known that such honesty has been taken as something like a personal affront. But difficult though it may be to attain this ideal, we must go on believing that it is worth seeking.

Simply to get people to talk is plainly not enough, for we must do our talking with a difference. It is not enough to remember that everyone must be kept in mind; our talking must also have direction. It must be talking, not to a fixed point known to the parish priest beforehand, as would be the case with a teacher and a junior class, but to a point in the unknown. The Meeting is a meeting of disciples, assembled to learn what is the mind of the Spirit, a 'not knowing whither he went'. Such ventures have obvious disadvantages, so that it is not at all surprising that many priests and people with some slight experience of what happens hastily return to the beaten tracks and the more familiar landmarks. Equally it is not surprising to hear from others that they had sleepless nights after the Meeting thinking over what had been said. This last remark, which points to real excitement of mind and spirit, is not so trivial as it sounds. A spark has been kindled into a flame.

What happens if people will not talk? What do you do if one person tends to monopolize the talking? In the first place we must recognize that we are doing something novel to the majority of our churchgoing people today. We have only to face this fact to realize what an indictment of our methods and what a formidable handicap to our work it is. Even today, after years of Summer Schools, Parochial Conventions, Missions, and the like, the majority of the people in our congregations are not accustomed to talk naturally about the Christian faith. It is true that there are arguments in the works, in the railway carriages, in the office, on religious matters, but it is noticeable that, apart from the intervention of some enthusiast, the discussion is carried on on an impersonal level. What nobody wants is the unpleasantness of getting 'personal'.

Consequently we must recognize that the awkward silence which so frequently overtakes a Parish Meeting in its earliest years is an indication both of our lack of training and of our ignorance. There is no easy answer to the problem. One parish priest who endeavoured to correct this by announcing that instead of a sermon there would be a discussion in church the following Sunday night, found the church empty, and later overheard the remark that 'he was paid to preach'. Others have struggled with the most difficult art of coaxing into life the beginnings of discussion over many months, and found that in spite of everything they tried a stodgy silence descended.

It is at this point that many have recourse to the practice of having a speaker. It is not unknown that some parish priests have worked out for a year ahead a rota of speakers and have printed a card to indicate their subjects. For many this plan has the obvious advantage of giving discussions a foundation of information and something to talk about. But the advantages are likely to be bought at too great a price. Valuable as it may be to stimulate discussion, and important as it is that we should hear the views of worthwhile speakers, it is likely to be disastrous if this becomes the usual procedure of the Parish Meeting. It is not too much to say that speakers should be asked to come in proportion to our strength and not our weakness in discussion. For it is true of both priest and people that when we are listening to a speaker, we are, with the exception of a few experienced listeners, more passive than we should otherwise be. To put it crudely, speakers are popular because they make it easier. We tend to sit back where otherwise we should be called upon to be wrestling.

In the long run therefore, whatever the immediate advantages of listening to a speaker, our job is something that we cannot leave to anyone else. Speakers can help us with information, with the stimulus of personal contact, with the honesty of their approach to their subjects, but our job remains when they have come and gone. Our growing together in common understanding and common acceptance of responsibility still turns upon our willingness to disclose our minds to each other in sincerity and truth. It is for this reason that hours spent in saying and listening to the most commonplace remarks and the most trite observations are never wasted, provided that we do not let them pass unexamined and provided that we wrestle with them. It is the job of the parish priest to ensure that this wrestling goes on. It will not happen if, in the earlier stages, he shows signs of impatience with those who seem able only to contribute platitudes. What matters is that he should be able and ready to sift the grain and chaff, taking infinite trouble to do so, and to see that the grain is examined and re-examined by those present at the Meeting. He may read more into what is volunteered by someone than they dreamt of. Nevertheless it is his job to encourage the timid and reserved to make their contribution, and himself to realize that nothing is so encouraging as the knowledge that our halting contribution, so diffidently offered, was genuinely welcomed and used. A personal knowledge of the people who attend the Meeting must be the guide in deciding whether the encouragement of some particular person shall take the form of a direct question: 'What do you think about that, Jack?' or whether we throw out the questions generally and catch the first reply.

Still more will turn upon the attitude of the parish priest as leader. In view of what has been said of the character of the Meeting, it is plainly not his function to give the impression that he thinks he knows all the answers, or that this is a glorious opportunity for delivering a lecture. His steering, his interrogation, and his sifting must all be done as by a member of the Body and not as by one set over it. The atmosphere of the family and the completely informal approach to the whole business of the Meeting must go hand-in-hand with an obvious desire to learn and a willingness to act upon what is agreed.

This last point is mentioned here because it has a great bearing upon the question of the survival and growth of the Parish Meeting. It raises the whole problem of what participation in the Meeting is going to mean. We are asking people to regard it with the utmost seriousness and to come into it as wholeheartedly as possible; to drop a good many of the usual barriers of social small-talk, and to speak honestly of the things that concern them most. Seriousness does not mean severity and gloom, but it does mean a recognition of the fact that we are not talking for talking's sake. Quite quickly the people present will ask themselves whether the parish priest who has called the meeting as an assembly of the Church, the Body of Christ, the Temple of the Spirit, does really mean what he said about it. Does he, for example, take seriously what is said there, does he think over it, as he expects the parishioners to think over what he himself has said? Does he intend that the Church should act upon what is decided, or does he go his own way when all has been said? The complaint has been made already many times: 'He says that he wants to hear what we think, but he never acts upon it; we might just as well have held our tongues.' Actually the outcome of this kind of thing is even worse. People rightly resent being called upon to do something which is costly to the sensitive-minded unless they can be assured that it is rightly valued. They are quick to detect a note of superficiality and humbug.

> Why didst thou promise such a beauteous day
> And make me travel forth without my cloak?
>
> Sonnet 34

It is not too much to say that the position of the parish priest in this respect is vital to the right understanding of what the Parish Meeting stands for. Humanly speaking, everything turns upon his integrity and sensitiveness. He can help the Meeting to go forward to hitherto quite undreampt-of levels of understanding, spiritual insight, and adventurous courage, changing the whole outlook and will of the Church, or he can fritter away the time, the resources, and the confidence of his people. One of the earliest signs of what is happening will be found in the way in which people respond to this opportunity to speak. There is a world of difference between the silence of those who are thinking and the silence of those who are merely waiting for someone to say something.

TOPIC FOR DISCUSSION

'What do you find to talk about?' The question is so often asked by those inquiring about the Parish Meeting that something must be said about it here. It is, of course, a little astonishing in view of our admitted concern for the whole of human life to find that ordinary churchgoing people should doubt whether we can find enough to talk about. Our real difficulty is to find the time to face half the things that are there to be discussed. There are, as Uncle Pumblechook remarked, 'Plenty of subjects going about, for them that know how to put salt on their tails.' How then is the agenda to be put together?

The answer is simply that we must let it be formed by actual experience. It must grow out of what is facing the Church internally and externally on every front. This means that there is no aspect of the Christian life, no problem that faces the Church, no project or campaign that we are asked to undertake, that should not be discussed at the Parish Meeting. In so far as the Church is alive and active, the Meeting is the clearing-house of its activities; in so far as it is trying to ground itself in the deep things of God, the Meeting is the solemn assembly where inquiry and wrestling go on. It rests with the parish priest to see that all aspects are kept in view. Let us take for example two actual agenda papers of a Parish Meeting.

A

1 Half-hour discussion on the work of William Temple, using Canon A. E. Baker's Pelican book as material.
2 Half-hour discussion on recent talks given by the Bishop of the diocese on Christian Morality.
3 Reading of a short article from the Diocesan Review on the situation in China.
4 Planning of the approaching Whitsuntide procession through the parish in which members of the Church were to portray the contribution of the Christian Church to the life of Britain.

This last item covered many weeks and involved drawing up a programme, a leaflet for distribution in the streets, and a good deal of fact-finding about the life of the Church.

B

1 Reading of a letter from a priest working in Trinidad.
2 Report of a recent visit of one of the Church members to a group of small country parishes, leading to discussion of the special problems involved.
3 Preparation for the monthly Parish Breakfast (a routine matter).
4 Lengthy discussion of the annual report of the National Council for Civil Liberties, with special attention to the position of the BBC, the state of the law affecting the mentally handicapped, and questions of freedom of speech.
5 Whitsuntide procession, further arrangements and assignment of jobs.

These brief notes of what was actually done on two consecutive

Wednesdays, recorded in the log-book, suffice at this stage to
show how parochial affairs and local business are handled along
with the world-wide affairs of the Church and the problems of
our common life. It is surely important that members of the
Church should be helped to overcome the narrow departmen-
talism which plays havoc with our witness and to grow in
informed concern for all these different aspects of the common
life. It is equally important to emphasize at this point that a composite agenda in which different ranges of experience are
touched upon is valuable in helping to bring into the activity of
the Meeting all kinds of people who otherwise might sit silent.
Just because the Parish Meeting is meant to include all ages and
all types of people, we must recognize the need to vary the
topics, even when a few enthusiasts are keenly developing their
particular subjects. We must learn to talk in such a way as to
bring all kinds of people into the field of talk, to be able and
ready to give the right kind of illustrations which will help the
others to follow. Once again it rests with the parish priest to
notice the trend of the Meeting and to be ready to pass from one
item to another when the 'feel' of the conversation requires it,
not by an obviously arbitrary closure, but by inviting attention to
other aspects.

One of the commonest things to occur at the first few
Meetings, whatever the declared agenda, will be the 'grousing',
and airing of grievances. There are few parish churches in the
heart of whose life there do not exist unresolved problems and
long-standing difficulties, which are rehearsed frequently
enough in conversation but never faced by the Church. It is here
that we touch upon one of the most important functions of the
Parish Meeting. To speak of it as a safety-valve is to do less than
justice to it, for we are concerned with human and not with
mechanical affairs. What more important thing for the health
and soundness of the Body could there be than the opportunity
to bring these problems to light and patiently to unravel them in
an atmosphere of Christian concern? It does not follow that the
aggrieved will necessarily be satisfied, but it is likely that after
one or two repetitions in public of the ancient grievance, the
sting of rancour is removed and openness creates a healthier

attitude towards it. It is important, then, that there should be no attempt to clamp down upon this feature, which can loom so large in the earliest experiences of the Meeting.

Equally important and troublesome is the feature noticed earlier, when two or three people tend to do all the talking, quite often upon narrow issues. There are those who apparently cannot endure a momentary silence, and must for ever be talking. No sooner is a subject for discussion announced than they rush in with a handful of newspaper clichés. There can be no question of silencing such people or dealing abruptly with rather trivial remarks. They must be heard, and heard with sympathy, until it is reasonably clear that they have had their opportunity, and that the Meeting means to go further. The more good-humoured the breaking in upon their garrulity can be made the better. Indeed it is important that quite steadily through the growing life of the Parish Meeting, occupied as it is with the most profound and sacred matters as well as the most troublesome of our problems, we should learn to laugh together and develop the gaiety of spirit of a good family. There is no better corrective to the faults of the garrulous and the conceited, the cynical and the over-pious, than the good-humoured laughter and interjections of the other members of the family. This can only be achieved if from the beginning we avoid set speeches, refrain from standing to address the meeting, and refuse to develop a heavy formality about procedure. Most Church discussions still contain far too much pomposity, and the Parish Meeting has a good deal to do by way of deflating it.

At the same time, we cannot lose sight of the problem of strained relations, quarrels, and open antagonisms. The more strongly we feel about our cause and the more vigorously we act upon our beliefs, the more certain we are to offend others. The more closely we are knit together in this Christian community the more keenly we can be hurt and hurtful to each other. It would be absurd to suggest that simply because we held a Parish Meeting we could root out all these problems. Indeed, the Parish Meeting would seem at certain times to be positively productive of such troubles. But the gain from the meeting is a very real one. The important thing is that the tensions that arise should be known and dealt with by the whole body of the Church, not as extraordinary affairs, but as part of the workaday life of a family.

One other feature of the practical working of the Meeting may be mentioned here. In meetings of Church people discussions are carried on far too frequently in 'ideal' terms. Speaker after speaker will talk eloquently of what might be done, of good suggestions we might entertain, of Faith and Power and Sacrifice in vague and hopeful ways. Discussions are held on which there are all too rarely investigations to discover what has been done. How often, for example, do we check the results of an evangelistic campaign? How much do we know of the outcome of the Report *Towards the Conversion of England*? It is, in consequence, one of the weightiest duties of the parish priest to see that the Parish Meeting is delivered from this snare. It can be done if, in each discussion where proposals are made, the Meeting is trained to be severely practical in examining them and to realize that what is said about the Church is being said about the body actually assembled. There will be much less said in terms of the Bride of Christ, and much more in terms of household duties. Although we have emphasized the fact that the importance of the Parish Meeting does not depend so much upon the making of plans as upon the communion of spirit and understanding gained, when plans are being made the Meeting should be more and not less practical than so many meetings, just because it realizes its calling to be the Church. There is no need to take votes. It is far better to work upon the 'sense of the Meeting', and make it quite clear that the utmost importance is attached to common action.

PRACTICAL DETAILS

Does the Parish Meeting 'take' in town and country parishes alike? The question is of great importance for many reasons. We need constantly to be reminded that the problems of the great multitude of thinly-populated parishes are not less exacting than those of the towns. We need to be able to deal with the remark that, while the Parish Meeting may be very good and helpful for some parishes, 'it wouldn't work with us.' Leaving aside for the time being the question of 'helpfulness', it should be clear from what has been said already that since information and flexibility are two of its most necessary features, there is no reason why the actual running of the meeting should not be capable of almost infinite adaptation to meet local needs. If we argue that no two parishes are alike, we can be just as ready to affirm that no two parish meetings need be alike. Indeed a great part of our present purpose is to suggest that groups of Christians should come together in their different parishes and set to work to find out what is the shape and nature of the Church in that place, without any requirement that it should conform to a pre-determined pattern. Nevertheless it can help the others to hear about what has already happened in the attempts that have been made.

In the first place, it should be made clear that Parish Meetings have been working in all kinds of different parishes. The writer has joined in the work of such a Meeting for two years in a cathedral city, for five years in an unemployed mining village, and for nine years in an artisan parish in Sheffield, and has been present at Meetings in tiny villages, colliery towns, residential suburbs, and in the heart of London, covering something like thirty parishes. A great many more parishes have developed their Meetings of which we have no first-hand knowledge. The outstanding fact is that the Meeting has been adapted to meet all these different needs.

No doubt we are made more conscious of certain problems in the smaller country parishes by the fact that only a few people may come together. The proportion to the local population and to the churchgoing population may actually be higher than it is in the big town parishes, but the fact that perhaps no more than two or three people come along does present us with special problems which must be faced. They will not be faced without a high conviction that the re-creation and rediscovery of the nature of the Church by two or three is infinitely worthwhile, and without the patience and the courage to sustain the effort.

One other comment may be made which concerns town and country alike. At some stage in the ebb from churchgoing and Church membership, we meet the man or woman who is inquiring about the Christian faith. To what do we direct them?

Where may we assure them that they will meet the Christian
Church? It is the conviction of those who have known the Parish
Meeting for any length of time that it is to this Meeting that we
should ask them to come. Let them come for months, if need be,
before services are ever suggested. Let them be encouraged to be
as critical as possible, let them be as searching as possible of the
quality of the Meeting, remembering the remark in the Report
Towards the Conversion of England, that 'the ultimate evidence for
the credibility of the Gospel must be a quality of life manifested
in the Church which the world cannot find elsewhere.' There
have been those already who have said that they could see the
value of the Meeting but not of services, and it may well be that
for a long time we shall get no further than this. But how great
a thing this is! Because there are people who are not ready to
'make Eucharist' with us, we must not lose sight of the immense
area of the common life in which we can enter into the mystical
union. The recovery of the corporate Christian life is actually
taking place when the twos and threes discover a reality in the
Meeting which they cannot now find in the services. Only here
can the prejudices and misconceptions and misgivings about the
Church, which are widespread and deeply entrenched, be freely
raised and frankly dealt with.

It is for this reason that in discussions upon evangelism we
constantly return to the experience of the Parish Meeting. 'We
testify to that we have seen.' Over a number of years new people
have steadily come in and taken an active part in the learning
and working life of the Body, have become new people in outlook and concern, have become witnesses in themselves to the
converting power of the relationships set up in the Meeting. One
of the problems of evangelism is the absence of this evidential
fellowship in the life of the local Church into which the new-
comer may be brought. Certainly the Parish Meeting meets that
need. But our contention goes much further. The Meeting is
itself the strongest and most effective 'sign' we have. Of this we
are ever ready to say, 'Come and see.'

With this in mind, we pass to the actual conduct of the
Meeting. What happens? About 7, 7.30, or 8 p.m., according to
the habits of the district, people begin to arrive in two and threes

and meet each other in the atmosphere of a home. There are no ranks of chairs arranged to face a platform; instead are the indications that we are gathering round a fireside. Cups of tea and an occasional sandwich or cake will help to make each member feel at home and able to help. Here too are the opportunities and the responsibilities of seeing that newcomers are welcomed and talked with and introduced. How much depends upon that kind of readiness to take such trouble, a multitude of people who have come into and gone out of our churches will bear witness. It is so easy to be friendly with our friends. 'But why is it', wrote one Christian, 'that the first six months in a new parish can be the loneliest time of one's life?'

When it is time to begin the discussion (the Meeting has begun as soon as people were arriving), the parish priest from somewhere in the middle of the gathering may ask for attention to the things the Meeting has to do. Some notices of forthcoming events may lead at once to the question of preparation for them, and this is one of our most important jobs. We spend a good deal of time attending meetings of various kinds, yet how little time is spent on equipping the members of the Church with the knowledge, outlook, criticisms, and requirements of the Church! How rarely can the speaker at such meetings say, 'We have discussed this thoroughly in our Church.'

Two illustrations of the importance of this kind of preparation may be given. In one case a Government official was explaining the reasons for a decision which affected the whole life of the nation. It was a large meeting, but when question time came no fewer than a dozen Christian people, men and women, were ready to ask valuable and searching questions which had been prepared carefully in the Parish Meeting the week before and which made the public meeting much more than a random battle. It is not too much to say that if the Christian Church took seriously this preparation of its members, to help them to have 'a right judgement in all things', the nation's public opinion would be vastly changed. As it is, the Christian is rarely heard and is rarely expected to have thought out his attitude to problems other than gambling, divorce, and Sunday games.

In the other case, the meeting was arranged by a Deanery

Missionary Council with a speaker returned from India. After
his address had been given, the questioning by those who had
spent some time preparing for the meeting so impressed the
speaker that he exclaimed: 'Had I known that you would have
come prepared to ask such questions, I would have cut my talk
and dealt with them at once. Why don't more people do this?'
We cannot but admit that much time and energy is wasted in
public meetings of the Church because we cannot assume that
those who attend have come with any reasonable preparation.
Where a Parish Meeting has done its work, it is undeniable that
its members stand out in the gatherings they attend as alert listeners and active participants in the discussion, simply because
they have gone equipped.

In the same way there will be opportunity in the Parish
Meeting to report on what has happened, for here again it is
notorious that many valuable discussions either never reach the
majority of people or reach them in a distorted fashion through
the press. Valuable reporting-back is a difficult art to acquire,
but training and experience in it is something that the Parish
Meeting should be giving to its members. Only by such a foster-
ing of alert participation in the wider affairs of Church and
State can the local Church be freed from the merited gibe of
'parochialism', and can its members begin to see what it means
to uphold Christian convictions in the different contexts of
modern life.

These items passed, there are many more to consider. It helps
to have definite questions bearing on Christian life and work.
Some examples of questions addressed by the Bishop of
Sheffield to the parishes of his diocese may be given:

1 What kind of community should a Christian Church be, and
   what should be its aim and mission in your town and parish
   during the next five years?
2 In what ways can this mission be made the corporate responsibility of laity as well as of clergy, in which each must share
   and all act together?
3 What more do you think should be done than is being
   done through worship, teaching, evangelism, and parochial

activities, to make Christ the accepted Lord and master of one and all, and to proclaim his Gospel?

4 What additional resources in clergy, workers, and equipment are needed? What are you doing to seek out likely leaders and to train them?

5 What changes in worship and in times of worship, in the provision of teaching and in other ways are necessary?

6 How do you see the relation between the Church in your parish and its task in the diocese, the nation, and the world? Is your congregation taking its share of the common responsibility?

To such questions as these we can come back repeatedly through the years, finding new stimulus in them.

From these we pass to the consideration of points raised by people in the Meeting. The workers in offices, shops, and factories, the women in homes, shopping queues, and with social contacts, are daily encountering the moral and spiritual problems of our time. What should they do? What should they say? We expect them to bear witness to their faith in these loneliest positions. It is right and proper that we should be ready to take immense pains to equip them for this task. But do we do this? Do we do it in particular ways and in respect of particular problems? It is precisely because the parish priest can never go into so many of these sections of the battle that he must call upon the laity, who do, to make known the problems that are to be faced. It is in facing these, not moral generalizations, that we fight our battles. It is in the day-to-day encounter and in the language of the people that replies must be made. No one can help better than the assembled Church, and time is never wasted if we can face real problems in this way and encourage people to bring them forward.

One or two examples may be quoted. One member present is engaged in welfare work in a large industrial plant, where large numbers of cases occur of fragments of steel getting into the eyes of the workers. To remove these with the care that a proper estimation of the value of eyesight demands may mean the loss of considerable time off work. The management is bent upon production, the worker may have been grossly neglectful of safety precautions, eyesight is a God-given treasure and responsibility – to what standard then is the welfare worker to pay regard? Even to talk over these problems in the mixed gathering of the Parish Meeting is a great gain.

Or again we recognize that the country as a whole is riddled with and perplexed by the habit of pilfering. Almost every worker can give evidence of what is going on. Men and women are taking home with them, with no great moral concern, whatever they can safely smuggle out of the works. Railway carriages are daily being stripped of electric light bulbs. What is the remedy? One worker present suggests that the management should make it known that they are ready to sell at cost price to the workers the articles they make, which vary from sandpaper to table-knives. Is that a reasonable, if limited suggestion? Another tries to go deeper into the causes of pilfering, knows what the pilferers themselves say about it, and puts his finger on Army life and habits of 'scrounging'. Another goes back to the question of the home. It hardly needs saying that we do not arrive easily at conclusions, for part of the value of this background of mixed experience is that it drives us away from too slick an estimate of the nature of the trouble. But what we do arrive at is bedded deeply in actual living.

A period of two hours a week is an extremely short time in which to face the questions that such problems raise. Meetings over several months may well be occupied with them. But other things, equally important, are demanding attention.

Almost every week the alert parish priest sees pamphlets, letters, and books which concern our Christian life. It is probable that in most parishes he is the only person who does see them. Unless he brings them before the Parish Meeting, they will never be known to any of the parishioners. The ordinary man or woman has no clue to their importance and no standard of judgement about them. How often, for example does the parish priest find in the course of visiting that pamphlets hawked from door to door have been bought because they appeared to be 'good', but chiefly because the buyer had no possible background of judgement. Knowing that it is not enough simply to select the best of these things and put them on a bookstall in church, the job of the parish priest is to make selective use of them in the Parish Meeting, to encourage the reading and *criticism* of them, bearing in mind that the majority of people have not begun to know what 'adult' education means, in secular as well as religious matters.

There is an enormous leeway to make up. At this point our main job is to find out how to make the best use of the material. Experience shows that well-intentioned reading aloud of pamphlets is one of the surest ways of killing interest. Few pamphlets and fewer books will stand this test, and this is not the way to use them. It is necessary that the parish priest should do a certain amount of pre-digestion, learning as he goes along how to transpose the written into the spoken word, to adapt the writer's logical development of his theme into questions, and to acquire the art of vividly summarizing the whole.

Does this sound as if it makes things too easy for the rank and file, too burdensome for the leader? Actually it is but part of the necessary preparation that any teacher must make for his job, and in this realm of adult education we are only just at the beginning of a quite tremendous project. Few people in our congregation follow the line of argument or even see the full force of illustrations in the written language of books and pamphlets. It is not that they are less shrewd and intelligent than the writers; but they think in a different way, and only rarely do they find a booklet written in their way.

A useful way of testing this is to set the Parish Meeting to write its own leaflets and to compare them with the more professional efforts. Certainly it will convince the parish priest that he needs to be very sparing indeed of extensive reading aloud from even the liveliest and most informative pamphlet.

To mention the writing of leaflets by the Parish Meeting is to embark upon another sphere of activity. The suggestion may strike the reader as absurd. How can we expect, for example, a group of people who, as we have already said, have a very limited understanding of what they read in books, to plunge into the more difficult task of writing? It is this very fact, that most people get so little out of pamphlets, that emphasizes the importance of trying to write our own. It is a commonplace that we learn more from our own efforts than from those of others. What is needed then is simply the stimulus of someone who will propose the subject touching some aspect of our Christian life and invite those present to suggest their own ways of developing the theme.

Group composition, for example, of a leaflet upon Baptism for use in the parish can be a more effective way of teaching or learning what we understand by Baptism than scores of sermons. Faced with the task of explaining something to friends and neighbours in language which they understand, and knowing so well what is commonly believed, most of us very soon discover how little we know of the subject, and how ill-prepared we are to give an account of our faith. These compositions, though they will never be literary successes, will nevertheless be of immense value in training the Parish Meeting to know what the Christian Church does stand for.

It may be objected at this point that there is considerable danger of the Parish Meeting becoming so engrossed in its own activities, so turned in upon itself, as to be quite arrogant in its judgement upon the work and life of the Christian Church as a whole. The danger is a real one, especially if in the course of public discussion those trained in the Parish Meeting discover themselves to be better equipped and better trained to hold their own. There is obviously a danger of becoming 'superior' and even of talking as if the holding of a Parish Meeting made all the difference between profitable and unprofitable discipleship. There is a temptation to regard the home-made product as being without any doubt superior to anything that anyone else might conceivably produce. The correction of this lies, not in crying down the local effort but in extending our knowledge. The position of the parish priest is in this respect a key position. It is his job to keep the balance between a continual incitement to more and more local effort (thus sustaining the conviction that it is of real importance), and a generous acceptance of traditional experience and wisdom derived from elsewhere.

One other feature of the ordinary Meeting we have tried to describe demands our attention. Coming into a session of a well-

established Meeting, we may be curious to know how homo-
geneous this gathering is. Experience suggests that, over a very
few years, the composition of the Meeting changes as new
members join. The consequence of this is that it is continually
necessary for the elementary lessons to be frequently rehearsed.
Otherwise we run the risk of newcomers getting no chance to
become acquainted with those basic matters by virtue of which
the Meeting has come to its present maturity. To go over these
things again and again requires no small degree of patience, but
the strength of the Meeting undoubtedly depends upon our
willingness to do so.

How then does the Meeting end? Every variety of ending can
be contemplated, but there are two things that experience
confirms as valuable. In the first place, it is useful to have a sum-
mary of the discussion, given as briefly as possible. Otherwise,
after a fairly long discussion, there will be many who go away as
confused by the divergent views they have heard, and likely to
announce that the Parish Meeting only left them 'more muddled
than before'. One of the beneficent activities of the Meeting
may be to break down the too rigid, unexamined, entirely 'all-
black or all-white' conceptions that exist in the minds of many.
It is equally true that the Meeting should help people to clarify
their minds and stabilize their convictions. To do this, it is not
necessary that every Meeting should somehow be pulled into the
support of a resolution, or that some neat and tidy declaration
must be produced if the Meeting is not to be described as a failure. But it is clearly desirable that the parish priest should point
to some of the most significant things that have emerged from
the discussion, and to tie one or two of them together so that
they present a reasonably ordered train of thought. All this must
be done quickly and unobtrusively or it is better left alone. It is
not an art that can be easily acquired. It calls for the whole of a
man's attention throughout the Meeting if he is both to follow
each turn and twist of the discussion and to arrive at certain distinctive points at the end.

Secondly it is desirable that before anyone leaves the Meeting
that there should be time for prayer. So far we have said nothing
whatever of praying in the Meeting. There are Parish Meetings

which open with hymns and prayers in church or in the room used for the Meeting. There are others which do none of these things. The chief aim should be the right ordering of what is done in the Meeting by setting it all in its most natural and simple relation to God in prayer. There may be times in the middle of the Meeting when it would be most valuable to suspend our talking and to pray together.

It is certainly important that if we pray at the beginning or the end of the Meeting we should do it together, and especially that there should be no question of formality about it. At times it can be in perfect silence, at others extempore prayer that catches up the matters of discussion, at others a remembrance of the unity of the Body with some special recollection of those who are sick, distressed, or sorrowing, as well as of those other quite normal things of human life, of people starting to live in another parish, another house, another land, of men and women starting a new job, of boys going into the Forces.

The more clearly the sense of the family is given the better. There are obvious occasions when the Meeting can be called upon to offer its evening's work and join in saying: 'And here we offer and present unto thee, O Lord, ourselves, our souls and bodies, our lives and labours, to be a reasonable, holy, and lively sacrifice unto thee.' It rests with the parish priest to sense the mood and outcome and need of the Meeting and to lead it in prayer accordingly. It may be that a collect will gather up the whole significance of what has been said and done, but what matters specially is that, if we are to pray at all, we should so pray that the particular meeting with all its problems, purposes, happinesses, stumblings, should be related to the eternal Wisdom, Love, and Patience of God, and his Holy Spirit in whose Name and Power we meet.

SOME SPECIAL QUESTIONS

What place has Bible Study in the Parish Meeting?
The question can best be answered by drawing as fully as we can from actual experience. One evening we faced the matter in this way. 'Why do we do our Bible-study so badly? Why do we so

often find that a large number of people at once relapse into silence?' For the plain fact was that a slight feeling of unreality appeared to descend upon the Meeting.

Some explanation may be given by going back to what was said earlier about reading books aloud in the Meeting. Even the most ordinary reading-matter sets up a kind of barrier, and introduces a break in the conversation. How much more then, when what is read in the Bible language, when a traditional text-employing mode of usage has bedevilled the approach, and when there is a certain feeling that this is all remote from our world.

All these things are far greater difficulties than most clergy-men ever suppose. Their own education and training have been so largely literary and biblical that they find it difficult to imagine just how the man in the pews thinks of the Bible. They can be more natural in reading it and talking about it than the layman. They can read it with some of the necessary historical transposition and theological understanding that surmounts so many difficulties.

But the literal approach which so quickly shows itself in the Parish Meeting at once reveals the difficulties. We are studying, for example, the Sermon on the Mount. We encounter the remarks on our attitude to borrowers, and at this point one of two things is likely to happen. Either the difficult words are read and passed over without a remark, as if implying that of course we all know how to apply them to an importunate borrower of our acquaintance, or else some person, possibly the parish priest, breaks in and exclaims that this is not quite as acceptable to any of us as our silence suggests. In other words we are not really facing the difficulties. Because this book is the Bible we are passing over remarks of which we should certainly be more critical if we met them elsewhere. To make matters worse, it is common to find that, if we are challenged to say how we think that so many of these difficult things are to be faced, phrases like 'We must have faith' promptly make their appearance. As statements they may be unexceptionable, but they are often to cover up the most awkward gaps in our thinking. The result is that we tend to emerge from our time of Bible-study with a new note of unreality in our discussion.

To overcome this, it would appear to be more profitable to do our Bible-study in very close relation to the actual problems of the day, drawing upon the Bible as we go along for comment, rather than reading ahead chapter by chapter. It is useful, for example, to study a subject with Bible references, or to build up a vivid picture of the Ministry of our Lord, or even to work out the meanings we attach to phrases like the Kingdom of God. All this really requires great preparation on the part of the parish priest, not simply in order that he may know the text to be studied but much more that he may himself be faced with the difficulties it presents. When we spoke earlier on of wrestling, it was with the implication that this wrestling was a reality for everyone. The unreality which creeps into so much of our Bible-study is due as much as anything to the fact that while we have to work out the problems of daily life, the difficulties of the Bible are for so many of us academic and not vital to our lives.

The force of this is very clearly emphasized when we turn to a different problem, that of politics. 'Do politics come into the discussion at the Parish Meeting?' Since we began by insisting that all matters which enter our daily life are the proper concern of the Meeting, we can hardly avoid the wide range of subjects which have their roots in politics. To do so would be at once to excise from our programme matters of great concern to our social and personal life. The difficulties are very real, and we can appreciate the attitude which so often finds expression in forbidding 'Religion and Politics' from discussion because both these subjects produce a deeply controversial note. We have heard of one Parish Meeting which decided to do Bible-study because current topics were too controversial. Certainly it would be easier if we could avoid the tensions which politics set up, but nothing is really gained by running away.

What we have to learn is the much more difficult task of declaring and maintaining our differences in politics and investigating the roots of them, within the acknowledged unity of the Church. Something is terribly wrong if the Church is any one Party at prayer to the exclusion of the others. Common sense must obviously be our guide. We must neither run away from nor run madly into the turmoil which the political scene presents. There are times when it is inexpedient to press the political issues further; when it is much more advisable to turn to matters where common ground is more easily discovered, from which indeed we hope to return to the difficult patches with second wind.

What do you do then, asks one harassed priest, with one or two people who simply will not let things alone? There are always some who will drag in the political issues, no matter what we are discussing. The answer is that we must build our own reputation for fairness and for keeping to the point. It calls for all the wisdom and the courage we are likely to possess, and few things make it quite so clear that the Parish Meeting is of incalculable importance. For it is in the face of admittedly deep divisions derived from politics that we must discover our unity. But we can head off the person who drags in 'politics' every time by showing how willingly we can admit and face political problems some of the time.

One other aspect of this matter should be mentioned here. Apart from 'party' questions, there are many topics which spring from our social life today that can profitably be discussed as welfare matters which as citizens we are all concerned in. It is most useful, for example, to find out how the public bodies which administer the social services are run, to create a genuine concern for their efficient running, and to make clear the extent of Christian obligation in respect of them. It is all too often lamented that Church people have left these things to others far too much, and that not enough interest is taken by Christians in trade unions, local government, and the various civil welfare bodies. The charge is very largely true. One of the most important things the Parish Meeting has to do is to direct the attention of its members to these secular fields in which our obedience to God is to be worked out. This will not be done unless we are able to convince people of the obligation to extend our conception of the terms of Christian service. At all times, then, the windows of the Parish Meeting must be open to this secular world, and it is here that, if we are to have speakers to help us, we should make the best use of them. One social worker invited to the Parish Meeting was able to point out how much those working in one field of social service hoped that Christian people would take a more active interest in the work.

The field is nevertheless not quite as wide as we should try to make it. It is our job to help more people to see that things they have never connected with religion have aspects which we must not neglect. What does the ordinary congregation make of the arts? By this we mean not simply a concern for religious drama, music, and architecture, but much more a concern for what the artist in any field is trying to do. If, as we suggest, Christians are people who are sensitive and alive to values in life, they are presumably very much concerned with the extending and growing of these things. They are people truly committed to the job of making communication richer and fuller than it has ever been before. If real life is meeting, then the channels through which we achieve this meeting are of great importance. The arts are points at which our sensitiveness to life is heightened, and where our meetings are rendered more inclusive of spiritual values.

What then does our Parish Meeting do about them? Our experience suggests that from time to time we should discuss with the help of well-informed people what is being done by artists, sculptors, musicians, writers, who are breaking new ground in their work. One of the most valuable of such discussions took place when an artist in charge of a 'Design in Living' exhibition came to the Meeting and explained its purpose. It is when Christian people begin to see the importance of teapots that pour properly and drawers that do not jam that we begin to apply some of our standards to daily living.

It is with this application of the attention of the Parish Meeting to the aspects of daily living which are not yet commonly the subjects of Church discussions, that we return to answer the question of Bible-study. There can be no doubt whatever of its importance. The Bible contains our title-deeds. For that very reason we must be more and not less aware of the extreme importance of being frankly realistic in our study of it, and must refuse to be led away into any day-dreaming about it. Above all we must be really learners, ready to admit that hard sayings baffle us now as they did the disciples long ago. Because we have had the Bible in our hands so long, we have in a curious way become unconsciously arrogant about it. It does not come easily to us to admit that we do not know what it means at this very moment in this very passage. The Parish Meeting makes good use of its Bible-study if it constantly brings us honestly to admit the truth.

The relation of the Parish Meeting to the Parochial Church Council
There have been, are, and will be in the future some problems connected with this question which only a long experience and considerable wisdom can help us to solve. It should be understood, however, that nothing which is said or claimed for the Parish Meeting here is intended in any way to imply that Parochial Church Councils should be discarded or ousted from their rightful position. But what is claimed for the Parish Meeting is something that links us up with Pentecost itself, and with the holy and life-giving powers of God, so that the question we have to face is more properly how far the Parochial Church Council helps in the extension of our work, and how far the Sacraments, the Word and the Meeting help us in holding a Parochial Church Council.

There is every likelihood that a certain suspicion will greet the appearance of the Parish Meeting as being a kind of rival to the Parochial Church Council. To deal with that we must continually go back to our insistence that in calling the Parish Meeting together we are assembling the Church of God. The Church may delegate to some of its members particular duties and responsibilities. The Established Church will certainly need statutory definition of some of these responsibilities. In respect of these the Parochial Church Councils have clear duties to perform. But always there resides in the Church itself as the *Body* of Christ certain responsibilities which it may not finally delegate, and of which it may not be relieved by any statutory action. These responsibilities are laid upon it by Christ himself, and meeting in His name it accepts them. There need be no quarrel over the division of responsibilities.

This means in practice that the discussions at the Parish Meeting will do two things that have a bearing on the work of the Parochial Church Council. In the first place they will provide a far richer, more informed, and more alert Christian mind for the working of the Church and therefore do something which the Parochial Church Councils have never done to any satisfactory degree. In the second place they will make possible far more sustained and intensive discussion upon matters which affect the spiritual welfare of the parish than the Parochial Church Councils have generally given themselves the opportunity to enjoy.

When therefore the Parochial Church Council meets to transact its business, it does so against a background of more mature and more continuous thinking on matters that affect the parish than we should otherwise have. There is no reason why the Parochial Church Council meeting should not be held as a continuation of the Parish Meeting, especially as so many of the people who have taken their Christian membership seriously enough to take a regular part in the Parish Meeting are likely to be elected to serve on the Parochial Church Council. In practice, it has been found in one parish that the most convenient way of relating the two has been to hold a quarterly meeting of the Parochial Church Council following upon the usual weekly Parish Meeting, thus incorporating the agenda of the Parochial Church Council in the work of the Parish Meeting. Clearly there is no need to lay down any suggestion of fixed relationships, but simply to insist that the Parish Meeting is not an organization.

'Over the wall'

The danger that the Parish Meeting may become too engrossed in its own affairs has been noticed earlier on. The remedy must always lie in an insistence upon as wide a conception of the work of the Church as we can possibly develop. In connection with this, it is important that the fullest use should be made of the opportunities afforded by local relationships. There is a very great need that groups of parishes should learn to work together. They can do this only so far as they are learning to see the common task of the Church from a common point of view, and it is just this which is so often missing. No one supposes that the Church in England is suffering from the obliteration of parochial diversities, however much the machinery of centralization increases. But we canot rest satisfied with mere diversity of tradition and practice. What is needed is the chance to enable this rich diversity to contribute to a common inheritance much more vigorously than it does at present. It is here that the Parish Meeting can do important work. Bound to no particular tradition of Church practice, it can flourish and invigorate them all. It can, moreover, be the means of reaching out from behind the parochial boundaries to enable the people to take action together.

A start can always be made by holding joint Meetings to compare experience and to discuss common problems. It has already been found that such efforts to link up parishes in this way are immensely influential in widening the whole conception of the work of the Church. There is no need to have an elaborate agenda for such a meeting. Let one or two parishes simply pay a friendly visit to each other's Parish Meetings and see for themselves what is being done. Let them discuss what they have already found to be their greatest problems or their strongest resources. Let them attempt to draw up a plan of common action. What matters most is the discovery of the foundations of our common life.

DO YOU FIND IT A SUCCESS?

This question is so often asked by those who make inquiries about the Parish Meeting that it cannot be left out. It is difficult to answer it without first finding out what the inquirers mean. Too often, one suspects, they mean by success an undoubted increase in the Sunday congregation and a general sense of the popularity of the Meeting. Both these are good and pleasant things, but they are not the immediate test of the value of the Meeting.

The Parish Meeting is not a means to an end, and certainly not to such an end as that of doubling the congregation. It must first be recognized for what it is in itself, the assembling of the Church to realize what it means to be the Church; and in so far as the Church does this, the Parish Meeting is doing the thing we look for. Its further work is to press forward from this point and week by week to work out the implications of the Faith. But we can no more say whether it is a success than we can say whether the Holy Communion is a success. It is far better to confine ourselves to a discussion of what actually has occurred.

In the first place, those who come undoubtedly gain a deeper sense of the corporate nature of the Church. In so far as the work of the Meeting runs true, it is impossible to take one's place through several months and years in the work without growing into a very decided relationship towards it, and this on a level that no other line of action can give us. Its purposes have become ours, its life our own. We do not talk about this corporate life, because we regard it as life that needs no such qualifications. The Meeting is the focus and expression of it.

Secondly, there is corresponding gain in the knowledge of each other. In no other way could we hope to become so truly 'Christianly' acquainted with other people. It has been a familiar matter of experience for many who previously had seen each other in church and had only known each other by sight, to find through the medium of the Meeting a quite different quality of relationship. If the essential character of the Christian Church, the 'I in you, you in me' relationship is to be laid hold of, if the Holy Community presupposed by the Holy Communion is to be known, then we are almost justified in asking how else are we to realize what this means save through the opportunity of the Meeting. Nowhere else in the life of the local Church have we comparable opportunity to develop this experience of truly belonging to each other.

Even more clearly can we point to the undoubted gain afforded by the Meeting in respect of the work of the Church in the world. It has been said with justice that the failure of the Church to guide men in the field of morals has been chiefly due to the fact that in its corporate life at all levels there has been so little free discussion of all the problems. The pulpit can only help up to a point; and because we have not been ready to give help to lay people by lay people nor to elucidate the concrete issues faced by them in the factory, the office, and the shop, in some such gathering as the Parish Meeting, it is small wonder that they tend to be largely indistinguishable from the world. It is the special business of the Parish Meeting to make possible week by week 'the free frank discussion touching the relevance of our faith to daily life.' Nowhere else in the life of the Church have we such an opportunity to learn together the facts of the situation, the pressures of the world upon our fellow-Christians, their daily conflicts in the common faith, and the possible ways by which a Christian standard may be upheld. It is quite certain that there will be a difference of opinion, 'But if the Church is a fellowship in Christ, it should be able to carry within itself differences of opinion and the possibility of diverse judgements.' Times without number we have heard it said that an argument in the works or office had been raised, and 'I didn't know what to say.' The experience of the Parish Meeting has been that people have found themselves equipped to reply, because over months and years they have been grappling with these problems in the context of the Meeting.

We look forward, then, to the time when our parochial system is transformed by the formation of these groups of men and women who in the Parish Meeting have found a new vision of the Church to which they belong. We have confined attention in this handbook to the actual working of the Meeting, and left unsaid many of the reflections upon the significance of the Meeting which are borne out by this experience. To bring out of her treasures things new and old is the prerogative of the Church. Not the least of these is the beginning of a practical rediscovery of the meaning of *Koinonia* – the common life of the Body of Christ.

IO

ON THE DISESTABLISHMENT
OF THE CHURCH OF ENGLAND

Quod ecclesia anglicana libera sit
That the English Church may be free

What did, does, could, or should the freedom of the English Church mean to the ordinary man or woman in the parishes or pews in England today? That there is some confusion and disquiet about the subject must be admitted. Perhaps it has always been so. Perhaps that is the price to be paid for having a Church at all. Wonderful and sacred mystery indeed, the spouse and body of Christ, the sheep which he bought with his death and for whom he shed his blood, it is also a shabby spectacle of human arrogance, self-seeking, cruelty, and fear. For all its vaunted claims to a concern for freedom, is it not true that from age to age it has bound heavy burdens upon the souls of men and women?

Yet the question of its freedom continues to demand and command attention. Its very title-deeds, its Scriptures, warn this generation no less than all that have preceded it that presumptuous sins may be the reasons for its unfreedom, its disquiet, its dissensions, and its feebleness of purpose. They nonetheless continue to recall it to its mission and promise of spiritual endowment, bidding all that have ears to hear with and eyes with which to see to address themselves in penitence and hope to their task here and now in twentieth-century England.

Early in this century John Neville Figgis remarked upon 'the disinclination of the average opinion to admit that the Church has any real social entity or any standard of doctrine or discipline except that of the nation at large.' The so-called 'Free Churches' and the Roman Catholic Communion were not markedly different from the Established Church in being more independent of the lifestyle, thought, and behaviour of the nation at large. The 'nonconformist conscience' and the dissidence of Dissent had grown feebler in things bearing upon the major trends of national life. In a variety of ways churches assimilated themselves to the ways of the world and ceased to exercise an independent scrutiny of the political and social life of the English people.

To say that Figgis and a few older men of his kind were minor prophets is to remind ourselves of one striking feature in the biblical writings which I have called the title-deeds of the Church as a whole, being accepted as such even though written and addressed to people living in very different circumstances than those of Christendom and its successor States. It is a reminder that the Hebrew consciousness was religious in a way that of Europeans is not. Hebrew reflection upon the history of its people saw history as the act of God and their own experience of it as the unfolding or reflection of the nature and purpose of God. It fell to the prophets to make clear the nature of this purpose and to summon the people to both understanding of and co-operation with it. They had no social authority of political or priestly character but fulfilled their calling by requiring the nation to resist any and every attempt to break up the integral character of Hebrew religion by allowing any form of dualism – social, political or contemplative – to make religion simply one aspect of the life of the nation. It fell to Jesus of Nazareth to extend prophecy beyond that national reference and to direct it towards a global field.

Christian churches grew up in Europe to provide a dualist religion for a dualist society. They saved that society from disintegration whether in its forms of Christendom East or West, or in the emerging nation states. It was a not unimportant task, and it is no disrespect to the churches to say that they provided the glue that these societies required. They were worsted in their attempts to gain temporal power but were needed to nurture notions of loyalty and obedience to it. They were not without skills in so doing.

> God bless the squire and his relations,
> And keep us in our proper stations.

All is well if that is the Christian religion. But it isn't. The title-deeds supply abundant evidence of the prophets challenging the authority of all rulers, lay or ecclesiastical, in the name of God who cares for the poor, the dispossessed, the slaves, the strangers and aliens as much as for any of his people. He requires justice and mercy for them and he will not suffer his intention to be disregarded. In modern imagery, he has planted a time-bomb in all states and societies who choose to disregard his purpose. These worldly authorities may go to all lengths either to suppress, or win over by deceit, potential prophetic questioning, but they cannot win. To choose to serve any other intention but that of God is to invite self-destruction.

It is to be noticed that the prophets may be very unwilling to speak until driven to do so, and even ignorant of the religious bearing of their words. It is not unknown for prophets to be priestly, but the likelihood is that the great majority will not be. That has an unfortunate consequence in that churches rarely encourage their members to pay close attention to the voices of outsiders. If, for example, more notice had been taken of what poets and novelists and artists had to say, the churches would have been more imaginatively alive to what has been happening in the modern world when the industrial society and the post-industrial one came along. They would have been less frightened of those prophetic analysts of what was happening in European society and its spill-over across the world, and better equipped to speak a word in season regarding the health and salvation of the people of God.

Again, it may be said that it was no mean achievement to encircle the globe with missionary enterprise and thus to extend the range of that time-bomb. To adapt a phrase of Caliban's, a host of new peoples could begin to say: 'You taught the language and I know how to rebel.' The swiftness with which this has begun to happen is one of the striking features of the twentieth century. The Kairos document from South Africa and the numerous movements in Latin and Central America are excellent examples of it.

What happens in England is but a tiny part of this universal movement. The proposed disestablishment of the Church of

England, momentous as that must seem to those likely to be immediately affected by it, is not world-shaking in its nature, but it is as important as any other movement in the world as a response to the call to freedom of the children of God. The eyes of all God's people need to be opened. For that reason the state of affairs in our parishes and pews deserves attention. Who are we to accustom ourselves to prophetic demands?

One answer may be given with our title-deeds in mind. We can take a new look at our nation's history and try to catch sight or sound of prophetic witness in it. When we hear or see that, for what it was in the past, we may be better equipped to respond to it now. History does not repeat itself, but old sins come along in new forms and we can learn to detect them. It is commonplace to admit that England in the post-war period and notably in the past ten years has undergone a vast change in social, political and economic matters. Reactions to change likewise have marked similarities across the centuries. Something reminiscent of sixteenth-century anxieties as well as masterful pride is to be discerned in our contemporary conditions. 'Costly thy habit as thy purse can buy' is very much in tune with our consumerism. 'Whip me these sturdy beggars' accords with the cost-efficiency drives to regulate social relations. On the whole however we are so unaccustomed to using our English history to illuminate our spiritual condition that we have to work hard to make a start. William Blake devoted his life's work to it, but his history was too meagre for the purpose. Nothing less than a big effort to recover a detailed lively sense of the issues raised by our history will meet our needs.

Where then and how to begin? My title is taken from Magna Carta. It sounds magnificent until we start inquiring what meaning could be attached to an English Church, then or now. A well-informed description of the Church in England in 1215 would make it clear that it bears very little relation to the Church in 1715 or 1915 and 1989. We should be compelled to ask what is this Englishness that we affix to the Church and lay claim to.

I recall a Norwegian pastor whom I introduced to a number of churches in Sheffield years ago shaking his head to indicate that he was quite baffled to know what the Church of England was. Nikolaus Pevsner in his book *The Englishness of English Art* has likewise marvelled over its various features which almost defy logic in being held together, full of admiration of it though he was. Lytton Strachey suggested that it was the long strong fingers of Elizabeth I which gave the final twist to what had been growing for ages, deep rooted in the national life. Hence, 'Anglicanism has never produced – never could produce – a St Teresa.'

Possibly not, but sanctity is not limited to one form. The Church in England has had its saints, and it is to the saints that we go to mark and learn the lineaments of the Spirit at work in the flesh and blood of men and women. In their various ways they demonstrate freedom with an often shy but always stubborn determination to be themselves under God and not anyone else. Few of them were all-rounders, but all saints have their failings as well as their virtues.

I want to consider one of them in relation to this question of disestablishing the Church of England, and to do it from the angle of a parish priest's work – which is the only base that I have any lengthy acquaintance with. I had read accounts of the lives of several English saints, and through the Catholic Crusade had paid some special attention to one of them who, as an Archbishop of Canterbury, was not only martyred, but given a considerable place for several centuries in the popular devotion of English people, until on 16th November 1538 King Henry VIII issued a proclamation not only denouncing him but forbidding all mention of him in the calendar and service books and also all images and pictures of him. An unauthenticated story even reported that the body of the saint was put on trial for high treason and burnt in 1536. It is a story reminiscent of the way Pope Stephen treated the dead body of his predecessor Formosus.

Henry VIII would appear by any such accounts to have been sensitive to the popular acclamation of a man who had resisted royal authority. He had after all to deal with men of his own day like More and Fisher and some obstinate Carthusians. Bad examples were too dangerous to overlook. The insistence that the clergy should keep out of politics has a perennial note.

With this in mind, when the Bishop of Sheffield, Dr Leslie Hunter, came to the Church of Holy Trinity, Darnall (of which I was the parish priest) some forty years ago, to consecrate a new holy table and the furnishings of a chapel then in use for the weekday Holy Communion services, I asked him to dedicate the chapel in the names of Our Lady and St Thomas of Canterbury. Few people today object to a 'Lady Chapel', and though he murmured something very quietly about 'undue medievalism', he graciously acceded to my request. Few bishops had striven more vigorously to bring the Church of England into a vital contact with the problems of the twentieth century world more than Bishop Hunter, few more bravely supported the work of Bishop Bell of Chichester in all that he did for the Christians, clerics and laity, who suffered for their opposition to Hitler and the Nazi programme. Few were more sensitive and imaginative about the place of liturgical prayer in the life of the Church. I suspect that nevertheless he did not quite see the relevance of this martyrdom of Canterbury to contemporary Christian Europe and England, just as many would fail to see what it has to do with disestablishment.

Why do we remember the names of these saints at all? I might have replied as the vicar of a church dedicated to the Holy Trinity that it was Archbishop Thomas of Canterbury who 'immediately after his consecration ordered that that great festival day of the glorious Trinity should henceforth be kept in England on the first Sunday after Pentecost.' In 1333 this English usage was adopted henceforth throughout the whole Western Church by order of Pope John XXII.

But there was a great deal more to be said as touching the remembrance of the saints known to us or unknown, and of this man Thomas in particular, but it had to be worked away at to become meaningful in the lives of men and women in the Church, and through them, one hoped, in the lives of others. Disestablishment will do very little for us if we do not use it as an opportunity to recover a full sense of the living history of our Church, a Church free to use its spiritual resources to the fullest extent.

Primarily that is a matter of recovering a sense of presence.

Bishop John Taylor wrote in his book *The Primal Vision* that
'presence is the debt we owe to one another.' It does not mean
trying to have a mental picture of other people, living or dead,
but of letting them be present with us now by an acknowledgement with gratitude that they are there to be loved through what
has been called 'a long elucidation of the Spirit'. I see disestablishment as a step towards learning to live in the company of the
dead and the as yet unborn, becoming free men and free women
of the Holy City, with our Englishness no longer tied into those
politic knots that being a State-Church imposed upon us and
committed to the palpable falsehood that this Church was the
Church of the English people, which it never was from the days
of the Tudor establishment onwards.

The Holy Catholic Church is the Communion of the Saints
and all those called to be saints. To pray in its fellowship is to be
taken up in a process of transcending ourselves and gaining a
true sense of identity. Disestablishment may help us to stop pre-
tending to be who we are not and may commit us to a genuine
approach to discovering the real nature of the fellowship in
Christ:

> Whose spirit is this? we said, because we knew
> It was the Spirit that we sought, and knew
> That we should ask this often ...

Of course we do not have to wait for disestablishment to set
about praying in this way. It is rather that we shall outgrow
Establishment by taking it seriously. What the poet Wallace
Stevens reminds us of is extended by some phrases from Iris
Murdoch's novel *Nuns and Soldiers:* 'Our being spreads out far
beyond us and mingles with the being of others. We live in other
people's thoughts in their plans, in their dreams ... we have an
infinite responsibility.' This is, of course what the Hebrew
Psalter said throughout in insisting that our identity is formed by
the interaction of our personal lives freed from the false restric-
tions that those obsessed by their lust for power or their fears of
each other impose upon us.

I am keeping in mind how this is to be done in the parish, in
its thinking and praying and acting, as a responsible body. It

compels me to return to the matter of history, so that we learn that it is not the dead past that we are concerned with but the living purposeful action of God at work amongst his people. That was and is something that Jews have always known to be the very stuff of their calling. 'A Jew can feel himself to be part of history, without making any special effort. The rest of us have to work harder every year to keep up with history (Iris Murdoch, *Under the Net*). To be without the sense of history in matters of liturgy and prayer is to be without a necessary discussion of the thrust of God's Spirit in his world.

Since I have instanced the significance of St Thomas of Canterbury in such a context, I would add an illustration of how a parish church was helped to grasp something of this. In 1935 Bishop George Bell commissioned the writing and production of T. S. Eliot's play *Murder in the Cathedral*. The timing could not have been more crucial. Hugh Trevor-Roper once wrote: 'If we are to understand changes in human history we must always remember the importance of single generations.' How can one who lived through the 1930s, whose minds and attitudes were formed by the terrible events of those days, understand or be understood by men and women to whom the events are mere history, reduced to the anodyne prose of text books? Understanding can come only by the imaginative power supplied by great artists and poets, and it was this that *Murder in the Cathedral* supplied to those who saw it performed in theatres or in Canterbury itself.

Could it ever reach a down-town parish in one of the big industrial cities like Sheffield? It could and it did. A few years later Miss Pamela Keily began her work in Sheffield to produce religious drama with the men and women she could recruit in that city. *Murder in the Cathedral* was one of her earliest productions with a 'cast drawn from folk who would never dream of reading T. S. Eliot: Becket was a shopwalker who had never been in church except to attend a wedding. One of the Tempters was a youthful milkman.' It took hold of them and of their audiences. Becket's martyrdom involved them in the brutal tragedies of the world they were living in and opened their souls to the significance of what was taking place. Christians like Bonhoeffer

were being hanged, pastors and people beaten to death, and
their murderers were saying to the world those speeches which
the four knights made to the audiences in the second part of the
play.

> 'It was our duty,' said the third Knight.
>
> 'If you have now arrived at a just subordin-
> ation of the pretensions of the Church to the
> welfare of the State, remember that it is we who
> took the first step,' said the second Knight.
>
> 'This man, formerly a great public servant
> had become a wrecker,' said the fourth.

'If only the Church would keep out of politics ...' We hear it
said daily, and we still do not learn. It escapes the notice of many
still that the Established Church has been 'in politics' for some
four centuries on the basis of an expectation that it will be
always what its political masters require it to be.

But there is something more. Year by year on the two festivals
of St Thomas of Canterbury, 29th December and 7th July, at the
reading of the Scriptures appointed for the Commemoration of
Martyrs, I read a part of Becket's Christmas Sermon from
T. S. Eliot's play. 'A Christian martyrdom is never an accident.
Still less is a Christian martyrdom the effect of a man's will to
become a Saint, as a man by willing and contriving may become
a ruler of men. A martyrdom is always the design of God, for
His love of men, to warn them and to lead them, to bring them
back to His ways.'

We thought of the countless numbers of men and women
who have under God been just such workers together with God,
and who have laid down lives for his Kingdom. Compared with
them and in their light, Establishment is a poor shrivelled thing.
We need to take up our true inheritance again and claim our
freedom, bought at so great a price.

I I

ON LIVING OXYMORONICALLY

> A figure of speech in which apparently contra-
> dictory terms appear in conjunction. From the
> Greek *oxos* meaning 'sharp', and *moros* meaning
> 'foolish'.
>
> *Concise Oxford Dictionary*

I am tempted to say, 'Don't get alarmed.' On second thoughts I
hope you will, because oxymoron requires just that.

Let me explain. Our ancestors attached great importance to
'rhetoric' – the art of effective persuasive speaking or writing.
For various tricks of usage they had wonderful names like
anacoluthon, aposiopesis, and chiasmus. It made them very
observant and possibly more accurate than ourselves. Among
them, a favourite, was oxymoron, a figure of speech in which
contradictory terms are joined together so as to give point to the
statement or expression: for example, sharp and dull, sound and
silence, and, from Chinese cookery, sweet and sour.

Now the language of poets is full of oxymorons. Wordsworth
brings together 'blankness and intuitions', 'gleams of insight and
perplexity'. But I want rather to talk of something we all do in
our liturgy today – the Giving of the Peace. Not everyone likes
it or sees the point of it, and we have got to explore its
significance beyond grasping people's hands, greeting them,
even sometimes kissing them. I want to ask, What is the oxymoronical aspect of it? What of Jesus' saying that he came not
to bring peace but a sword? Ought we to wish someone that – or
take it from someone else?

If we are going to give the Peace – and I am becoming convinced that we need it – have we not to go back to the Gospels

and reflect and pray about it? Have we ever faced the saying, 'The Kingdom of Heaven suffers violence and the violent take it by force'? In these days we are rightly perplexed and horrified by the daily toll of violent acts, but I put alongside that fact those words from the Gospels, which formed an *opening sentence* in the liturgy I grew up with, and which were much used by one of the greatest and gentlest of the Roman Catholic martyrs in the reign of Elizabeth I. (He knew what they meant to him and died a hideous death uncomplaining.)

To return to the Gospels: 'Peace I leave with you; my peace I give to you; not as the world gives do I give to you' (John 14.27). 'I have said this to you, that in me you may have peace. In the world you have tribulation; but be of good cheer, I have overcome the world' (John 16.33). And the word translated 'tribulation' is the Greek *thlipsis*, meaning the pressure of the wine press or olive press.

Jesus is clearly speaking 'oxymoronically': peace and agony are being held together. The one thing the apostles were not going to get from and in the world was *peace*, either from the magistrates or from their own households and friends. He did not. Why should they? Talk about peace should not hide the disturbance that Jesus made. His enemies said that he stirred up the people, and they were right. If Jesus is Lord of all life, well, life is a matter of being stirred up.

So I welcome the gesture of the Pax, but I want it oxymoronically. How do we get that?

We shall not seek it or get it unless we face it in prayer and attempted living. But let me put it another way, to express it better. That great and wise teacher Unamuno wrote towards the end of his book *The Tragic View of Life*: 'God deny you peace and give you glory.' Harry Williams has translated it, 'God forbid you peace ...' I am not suggesting that we should literally tack these words on to the Pax, but I am saying that we should be praying to get hold of them so that they find their way into our living. After all, is not that the main point of the liturgy already?

Let us ponder the meaning further. In what other ways may we be required to live oxymoronically? Here are some words of Lowes Dickinson after he had suffered a grievous blow: 'There is a resentful querulous grief which throws the sufferer in on himself and makes him petty and tedious. There is a grief which expands towards the universal and generates action.' We have all seen something of that to know its truth. We know that grief is not to be treated superficially or stoically or evasively, but is to be related to the ultimacy of God, to the outpoured passion/compassion of God. Unamuno again: 'Those who believe in God, but without passion in the heart, without anguish of mind, without uncertainty, without doubt, and even at times without despair, believe only in the idea of God and not in God Himself.'

What grief threatens to do to us is to shut us in on ourselves when its true value is to set us free to go beyond what we have been. Consider the apostles' grief at the death of Jesus, and then the possibility that by belief in him they could participate in his true life. Their grief must be the ground-note for a great shout of praise and song of deliverance.

And this. If we are not grieving over the state of the Church today we ought to be. Back in 1916 Lowes Dickinson wrote: 'The Christian churches will not, I believe, ever recover any influence nor do they deserve to. The greatest crisis in history has found them without counsel or policy or guidance. They are merely echoing the passions of the worst crowd.' These are hard words, but with a good deal of truth. It would not be easy to maintain that the churches have recovered or gained influence in the intervening years.

The trouble is that this loss of place, of influence, can turn people's attention inwards. They get enclosed, if not in their own fat then in self-assurance, self-assertion, self-justification. They build walls of defence, fortresses, garrisons.

Now, to be oxymoronical, I have to say Yes, there is a sense in which churches are citadels, places where we can stop our feet from sliding and find ourselves steadied. But we are not to stay behind the walls. The Church's job is to give its life for the world, to find out how to do this, to enter into the world's griefs, troubles, and pains, at every level. So the picture of it must be one of more *precarious* living, more exposed living. To keep it from being amorphous it must have formal outline, but it needs a *membrane*, which, if I understand the word aright, means a covering, a skin, but one that allows things to get through selectively.

Ask yourself, Is the Church like that? Is it being nourished by being in the world or is its attitude querulous and resentful? Clearly a lot will come in that is disturbing and grieving, but if that can be received through the membrane rightly – which is the Peace – then the response will be glory. It will find that because it can glory it has been given glory.

Jesus rejoiced before his passion in the glory that was set before him. Is that the oxymoronic lesson that we must make our own?

12

THE BISHOP AND HIS
RELATIONSHIP WITH GOD

A preparatory article for the Lambeth Conference 1978.

Dear Bishop

Re-reading the service of your consecration I am moved to write
to you, not simply to wish you well, not just to inquire how you
have fared since its words were spoken, and certainly not to offer
you advice, but to think aloud with you as a fellow Christian
about one aspect of it, one that indeed underpins all the rest.

I do so simply as one of the many on whose behalf you yourself undertook your difficult job. It is, as all Christian life-
commitments must be, a completely personal thing; that is to
say, it is unintelligible apart from its relation to that communion-
in-love which Christian belief regards as the foundation and
quickening creativity of all that is, the Divine Nature itself. I
write because I feel that we all should try to see and pray for you
in your job as a matter of continuing personal concern, for it
matters a great deal not only how you yourself see it but how
each one of us does.

I am aware of the dangers that arise both for you and for the
people of God from making too facile and too presumptuous
distinctions about your office. The high dignity ascribed to it, the
vicariousness suggested by it, can be insidious temptations. All
too easily an impression can be given and allowed to take root
amongst us that there is, for example, one standard of holiness
for the clergy and another for those not thus set apart. The consequences can be disastrous. The peculiar function of *episcope*.
the very thing for which you were distinguished in that act of
consecration, may be submerged and lost to sight beneath a host
of less worthy considerations.

It would be wrong to blame bishops only for faults and
failures of this kind. They reflect so often what an unpraying
Church expects and shapes. What people desire of us weighs
heavily with us all, can even bend us, and there is good reason to
think in the light of much of Church history hitherto that these
expectations have not always been really helpful. What are they
like today?

One must ask whether we as a Christian people take enough
trouble to see this as a shared concern and try to keep clearly
before our eyes the basic matter of which I write – your relationship with God, and God's expectation rather than anyone
else's about the job you were asked to do. Certainly your consecration service emphasized that, but we all grow forgetful of
such things. The inspiration of the Holy Spirit then invoked for
you can so easily be treated as if it could be taken in a passive
way, a way which goes far to impede if not destroy personal relationship at all. Some of our troubles in Church history do
appear to have stemmed from that, and there is no reason to
suppose that we are all exempt from temptation of like kind
today. There are, no doubt, special pressures to commit these old
sins in the newest kind of way bearing heavily upon us now.

I am equally aware of those seemingly proper expectations
with which people commonly approach you, desiring you to be
an able administrator, a wise theologian, a conscientious pastor,
a man of prayer, an apostle, teacher and prophet. The lineage of
your task in history as well as immediate necessities make it
almost inevitable that this be so. You will not be alone in lament-
ing your insufficiency for all these things, and in respect of so
daunting an office it may seem almost inconsiderate of me to
press the claims of one thing alone. Yet I do so now because I
believe that all else turns on this.

I am speaking of your relationship with God. Clearly there is
a sense in which yours differs nothing from that of any other
child or servant of God. You stand with the rest of us in a perspective that makes nonsense of all human distinctions whatsoever and invests the least as well as the greatest with the one
glory that is his.

But having first quite properly humbled our distinctions to the dust, may we not then with like humility consider your setting-apart as a bishop an act of God? It gives you at once a distinctive character notified to us in a rite in much the same way as marriage presents us with a husband and a wife. Something new has been introduced into life. I cannot forget that the God with whom we have to do appears to take infinite delight in the diversity of his creatures, in the variety afforded to plants and men, to rocks and beasts, insects and birds. Episcopal purple may vie with finches' wings or the peacock's tail!

Nor can I ignore a much more important, indeed basic feature of Christian belief that may be described as the particularity principle. It says that God himself has come amongst human beings as a particular man at a particular time in history and in a particular place in the world. 'Get me a body' the Divine Lover has been described as saying on that occasion as if nothing in time or space must impede the purpose he had in mind. In these days when we have grown familiar with cosmic implosions as well as explosions, I can think of nothing so implosive as that taking of humanity by God in that particular body born of that particular woman.

In that light your own particularity as a bishop may be seen to be both credible and important. Whether it be scaled down from divine to human provision or scaled up from earth's concerns to heavenly ones, the truth remains that in being thus chosen and set apart you were given an authentic distinctive place in the Divine Economy. You are, if you will permit me to say so, one of the consequences of that implosion called the incarnation.

We should lose no time moreover in taking seriously and pursuing our particularity principle further, or we shall be, as I suggested earlier, beguiled into fastening our own expectations too quickly upon you. It is with his expectation of you that we must be concerned. Is it possible to particularize on this?

Let me say at once that I believe it to be important in Christian practice to do so, whatever the difficulties it raises. Implosions cannot be tidily arranged for, and the Bible quite often, and rather specially in its presentation of the apostolic ministry of Paul, keeps the implosive aspect well to the front, difficult as this must prove to be for religious institutions. God's continual rethinking and refashioning of the world has at various times been expressed in the very singularity of the man sent by him to effect it. The hour was matched by the man.

There is no fixed pattern then to make clear the relationship of a bishop to God. On the contrary it is held in the grip of that unpredictable thief-in-the-night syndrome of which the gospels warn us, and there is a particularity attaching to *episcope* from the Godward side which is a stark reminder to the Church in venturing to make men bishops that its true life depends at every turn upon revelation of a quickening relationship with God. Consecration does but begin a process by which a man is wedded to the service of God. Judgement, furthermore, in difficult times may not only begin with the household of God but with the bishops therein. It could well be, as the prophet Isaiah made clear, a searing experience. Events of the last few years in one continent after another have gone far to confirm that nearness to the fire!

But the particularity of bishops is not restricted to such singularity of men and occasions. I think that its true nature is more helpfully illustrated by the Neo-Platonic doctrine of 'signatures' which could regard every feather of a bird's wing, every leaf on a tree, in all its particularities as manifesting an identical form repeated generation after generation. As one modern writer has said, 'The holly leaf simply by being itself celebrates a spiritual order, just as, by an old compassionate doctrine, the simple man fulfilling his proper vocation, makes thereby an act of piety: *Qui laborat orat*.' It is of the unchanged, unchanging *forma* of your episcopal vocation that I am compelled to think.

Since bishops down the ages have appeared in a multitude of styles it is not easy to do this. What is the *forma* and whence is it derived? One must go back to the biblical account of that creative-redemptive activity in which the salvation of humanity is wrought to discern its lineaments. Only here shall we find a sufficiently firm basis for our conception of it. The writer to the Hebrews, late on in the process of reflection on it insisted that it was discernible in the sending of the Son into the world by the Father in the particularity of the flesh. The writer was at pains to make clear how different this *forma* was from those patterns of priesthood with which human beings were already familiar. The gospels are no less insistent that such sending was repeated by him-who-was-sent in commissioning his apostles for like purpose and intention. The Book of Common Prayer service at the consecration of a bishop can find no more exact description of the character to be observed than by emphatic reiteration of such sending. The *forma* is 'One sent' and its entitlement no less than 'As my Father hath sent me, even so send I you.'

Everything turns then on the implications of this sending. What, in the first place, was it for? It was for the world's sake, this world that God so loves. Whether we see it as a rescue operation or as a piece of going-ahead, it suggests that apostolic *episcope* is the continuing re-assertion in human terms, age after age, of the Divine anxiety for a world beset by dangers and imperilled by temptations, an anxiety such as a parent would show for the welfare of children, extending quite naturally to the minutiae of the equipment of those sent. 'When I sent you forth, lacked ye anything?'

This is not a poetical fancy but the assertion of an experience of travail such as attends all birth. The business of the bishop so sent may well be defined in the general terms of Divine comparison such as Jesus used when sending out the Twelve, but only the actual context into which they moved could reveal the kind of personal involvement required. It means, as a consequence, that we are to visualize the relationship with God as a process of coming up to him at the places which he has appointed. We shall look for the bishop not among those who stand like the Twenty-four Elders about the throne but in some particular place to which he has been sent, in a see where he has sat down, quite often one poetically described in medieval romance as 'a siege perilous' and more laconically today as a 'hot seat'. His relationship with God is not attenuated by this – he is not in exile from the royal courts – but is in the Presence simply because it is with the Exodus God that he has to do.

To say this is not to lose sight of the fact that he may lose his way. The essence of a personal relationship is that it allows and indeed demands a freedom of will. Only in coming to that place may he know in the existential terms of biblical knowledge what is rightly to be done, but the place itself is never neutral. 'Come over to Macedonia' sounds fine, but who knows what lurks there conspiring to seduce the one who comes? Would that the writer of the book of Jonah had told us what happened in Nineveh when the mission of Jonah got under way. What did it mean to Hosea to have to live with a faithless woman? In a witty passage on Bishop Creighton, Lytton Strachey wrote, 'The ironical fact was that those events happened to take place in a world where no clever and studious clergyman of the Church of England had any business to be. Sobriety, as he himself said, was his aim; but what could sobriety do when faced with such figures as Savonarola, Cesare Borgia, Julius II, and Luther? It could only look somewhere else.'

Mr Strachey was wrong. It is the business of a bishop to be in all places whither God would send him, however fearful, corrupting, appalling, they may be. It is his business if so required to look evil in the face and to withstand it, not to look somewhere else. In the very particularity of this or that fiery furnace the relationship with God that your consecration declared must take the strain. How that is to be done can only be revealed in that place. The New Testament insists that it is not a matter that can be prescribed for beforehand. We must count it as one of the gifts of God to our generation that we have been given some glimpses of that relationship dwelling amongst us in the experience of people like Bonhoeffer.

To this fact of place I would bring also the co-ordinate of time. A relationship with God the Eternal is not something impatient of the temporality of things but charged rather with a heightened awareness of their significance in the eternal order. *Episcope* means insight as well as oversight, and demands an attentiveness to the changing world that is not beguiled by appearances but is sensitive to the revelations of the finger of God at work. The 'clean heart' of the psalmist's prayer is something akin to an unclouded mirror in which the reality of God may be reflected and like those screens on which the tiniest particles of matter are traced. They simply cannot work if we crowd them with the presuppositions of yesterday's picture of reality.

Your relationship with God demands a stripping off of accumulated impressions valid enough in their day but likely to prove a handicap in the new times in which you have to live. I spoke earlier of being exposed and I can think of few more clear examples of this than one which requires so drastic a letting-go of things in which we have hitherto trusted. Nevertheless I believe that the particularity of your sending into specific circumstances does entail what St Paul experienced as a condition of blindness, the effacement of those well-known images of reality, in order that the new vision may be seen. Martin Buber put it starkly enough: 'Meeting with God does not come to man in order that he may concern himself with God but in order that he may realize meaning in the world.' Where meaninglessness threatened to triumph (and it is a constant threat) it has been the job of a man sent by God to embody a new meaning, even if it be no more than a heightened degree of suffering or mourning for things cruelly destroyed.

I cannot therefore see you and your brother bishops at this time but as men whose relationship with God is not to be described in mechanical terms of delegated or developed authority, but always in that condition of openness to God that he may print in you that new revelation of himself that is demanded by the new circumstances into which his children have come. 'New every morning is the love ...' but it needs human beings to notice it; and the nights which Jesus Christ spent in prayer made possible, I believe, his continuing discernment of the ever-new operations of that love. I have not so far even referred to your own prayers, but what I have spoken of in terms of your job does, I hope, suggest what shapes and energizes your praying. It is the very gesture of response that you make to being so sent. It is the necessary sifting or winnowing process through which you take a firmer hold on reality and make it apparent to others.

That this is a particularity specially significant of your office as a bishop today I am quite convinced. Not for many centuries has there been such a situation throughout the world in which men and women have felt so much in need of help from those whose relationship with God is quickening and sustaining and

capable of piercing the opacity of the world. It is the homelessness of men and women today that sets the problem, the alienation from themselves, from their handiwork, from their fellows,
from nature, that lends its intolerable weight to a condition
bereft of the theodicies which gave meaning to life in the past.
That homelessness was once ascribed to the Son of Man as
though to make it clear his identification of himself with human
beings who 'at sundry times, and in divers ways' would find
themselves overtaken by the darkness of a meaningless existence. For their sake he came, and to speak of him as 'being
without sin' is, amongst other things, an attempt to say that he
retained one thing which defined separation, the fact that he had
been sent. 'If there is meaning, it is unconditional meaning, and
neither suffering nor dying can detract from it.'

May I conclude therefore with this final comment upon the
nature of your relationship to God, to the God and Father of
Our Lord Jesus Christ. It is a relationship most specifically
described in terms of mission, and of mission raised to the high-
est term of personal involvement. I am bound to see this, though
it is grasped in different ways by the artist, the parent, the
teacher, the cultivator of the soil and a hundred others, as being
an acceptance of responsibility on your part of answering with
your life to those expectations which just because they are both
human and divine constitute the relationship itself. In one of
those great moments of insight which characterize the apostle
Paul, who quite rightly never ceased to ruminate upon the
strangeness of his own being summoned to such a task, he spoke
of the emptying, the *kenosis*, of the Son's glory in his coming as
Man. I can believe that he came to it not as a piece of theological speculation but as something to which his own experience
pointed him. He knew what it was to be thus emptied, to have
nothing left but the fullness of him that filleth all, and to find
that fullness in communion with him who sent him. Of his fullness have we all received, and we have received it in passing
from one to another the heavenly bread of such a relationship.
Apostolicity meant that, and means it still today.

I remember reading in the Life of Mother Janet Stuart the
words: 'I must never be bored, never be offended, never be busy.

To be busy is to be engaged in an occupation which makes it inconvenient to be disturbed.' I am suggesting that your calling has its particularity in this commitment to meeting God in conditions where all of us are tempted to take refuge in boredom or business. I am not suggesting that you won't have moments of transfigured living, but those are bonus points and not the stuff of your calling.

Yours most sincerely,
Alan Ecclestone

13

SHAKESPEARE, RELIGION AND POETRY

When I consider every thing that grows
Holds in perfection but a little moment;
That this huge stage presenteth nought but shows
Whereon the stars in secret influence comment;
When I perceive that men as plants increase,
Cheered and check'd even by the self-same sky;
Vaunt in their youthful sap, at height decrease,
And wear their brave state out of memory;
Then the conceit of this inconstant stay
Sets you most rich in youth before my sight,
Where wasteful time debateth with decay,
To change your day of youth to sullied night;
    And, all in war with time, for love of you,
    As he takes from you, I engraft you new.

Sonnet 15

O golden tongued Romance, with serene lute!
    Fair plumed Syren, Queen of far-away!
    Leave melodizing on this wintry day,
Shut up thine olden volume, and be mute:
Adieu! for, once again, the fierce dispute
    Betwixt damnation and impassion'd clay
    Must I burn through; once more humbly assay
The bitter-sweet of this Shakespearian fruit:

Chief Poet! and ye clouds of Albion,
   Begetters of our deep eternal theme,
When through the old oak Forest I am gone,
   Let me not wander in a barren dream,
But, when I am consumed in the fire,
Give me new Phoenix-wings to fly at my desire.

JOHN KEATS
'On sitting down to read *King Lear* once again'

A plea

that we try to see Shakespeare's work as a whole, very much as we have learned to read the New Testament, a rich perception of experience having spiritual significance, an experience of a bygone age with bearing on our own;

that we try to see it as poetic drama, a ritual enactment of actual experience, to which we must give loving attention because our own spirituality is being engaged;

that we try to see it as groundwork of prayer, to be used as we have learned to use the Psalms, having their own 'coercive charm of form';

that we try to relate it to the political, social, and religious uses of our own common life;

that we take from it the challenge to creative effort in our own time.

I

'Leave thy damnable faces and begin.' Where and how?

2

... tentatively, with something Santayana wrote: 'Religion and poetry are identical in essence. They differ merely in the way in which they are attached to practical affairs. Poetry is called

religion when it intervenes in life, and religion when it merely
supervenes upon life is seen to be nothing but poetry.'

Whence do both draw their strength? From the imagination.
It is as our greatest imaginative fellow-creature that I want to
look at Shakespeare's work.

3

... with his work as a whole, as much as we can absorb. We are
to read him again and again.

4

To many of his contemporaries he was 'my gentle Shakespeare'.
To one of them, Ben Jonson,

> He was not of an age but for all time.

5

But Ben Jonson knew, as Shakespeare also knew and said, being
a player and writer of plays, that the immediacy of such playing
demanded attention.

> Let them be well-used, for they are the abstract
> and brief chronicles of the time.
>> *Hamlet* ii.ii.526-8

For when 'a great poet uses the stories that have taken shape in
the fantasy of the community, and handles them with unusual
sensitiveness to the words and images which express the most
profound emotional experience of the community, and thus
gives them their full evocative power, he not only brings to con-
summation the religious experience of men and women, but
releases it to discover under the guidance of the Spirit how to
venture forward: to a new sense of obligation, commitment,
involvement ...'

6

So I want to reflect a little on some of the things Shakespeare discerned in his time, in the wider play, political, social, cultural, actually going on, how he mirrored them in the plays he wrote, so that then and now we may the better 'play out the play', because there are always many things to be said, as yet unsaid, as yet unattended to, not only on behalf of rascals like Falstaff, but everybody else, our actual and potential 'friends'. And I hope that has its proper Johannine ring.

7

I must begin from the here and now: that we live in a desperately sick society. We are all infected by it, for in this present century our world has lurched from one bout of sickness-disaster to another. The best we can say of it is that the worst that human beings have prepared for themselves has not happened yet. Kierkegaard said that 'the individual cannot help his age – he can only express that it is doomed.' Shakespeare understood that frame of mind, but held another view.

8

He did so because he stood nearer than we do – though he had no misconceptions about its precarious condition – to a notion of human society that we are *not* just individuals, that we belong to one another, and that cultural things – religion, morality, art, liturgy, drama, prayer – are socially conceived and nurtured, and in turn nourish the spiritual vitality of that society, and counter the impoverishment which sets in unless those resources are put to good use and added to. Shakespeare's plays, Donne's poetry, and the Authorized Version of the Bible were outstanding contributions made in those years.

9

The need was great. Any epoch of change imposes great strains on the spiritual courage of people. The swifter and more extensive the change, the more men and women are assailed by fears, bewilderment, perplexity, misgivings, even panic. Such was the Copernican revolution, not only in physics, but in all areas of life, including the religious and political. While the people of Europe were launched into a new era of history, they were also plagued by irrational fears that make for barbarity and cruelty and inhumanity.

I am suggesting that Shakespeare's work be seen as the counter-attack of the Spirit.

10

Where and how to start to look at it? Perhaps Sonnet 64:

> When I have seen such interchange of state,
> Or state itself confounded to decay;
> Ruin hath taught me thus to ruminate –
> That Time will come, and take my love away.

Or Sonnet 65:

> Since brass, nor stone, nor earth, nor boundless
>   sea,
> But sad mortality o'er-sways their power,
> How with this rage shall beauty hold a plea,
> When action is no stronger than a flower?

Can rage and ruin teach me to ruminate, that is, to pray, to face as honestly, imaginatively, bravely, and hopefully the situation, personal and social?

11

We can ruminate only on what we have already taken in, have gathered, have become aware of in the life we share in. Drama, like all the arts, is one means of enabling us to do this, and the

doing of it *is* praying. When we bring, by the most extensive
effort, to our experience the imagination and honesty of purpose that is the keynote of great art, we are praying. Simone
Weil said that 'prayer is the triumphant art of the human
imagination.'

So I am suggesting that we ruminate on Shakespeare's work
that we may learn the better to ruminate on our own time, situation, and experience.

> Carry with us no ears and eyes for the time
> But hearts for the event,
>
> *Coriolanus* ii.i.285

remembering Yeats,

> Hearts are not had as a gift, but hearts are earned.

12

Can we, maybe, learn to see like that?

> May I be so converted and see with these eyes?

So Benedick in *Much Ado About Nothing* (ii.iii.123).

The whole work of Shakespeare, fourteen Comedies, twelve
Tragedies, ten Histories, is an answer. You may see it in the relations of men and women, in the affairs of a people, in the souls
of men and women, in the disclosure of 'what a piece of work
is a man', 'how beauteous mankind is', in the tragic despair of
'it is a tale told by an idiot, signifying nothing', and in 'Ripeness
is all ...'

13

But 'ripeness' is the end-product of a process of maturing.
Where was it to be begun? Art and religion have to meditate on,
wrestle with, a reality not ourselves only. The poet must come to
terms with the harsh cruel reality of the social and political
order in which he begins to work. No artist works in isolation. To
communicate at all, poet or playwright must catch the mood,

resonate to expectations, find the language which society responds to, must anticipate what audiences will warm to as well as find their own meaningful intention.

Let us therefore consider in this context the batch of plays called Histories. They do not constitute Shakespeare's most important work, but these plays do have a bearing on my concern for religion and poetry. He could well have said of the historical past,

> I grant thou wert not married to my Muse,
>
> Sonnet 82

but he nevertheless sought it out. Why?

14

Where Shakespeare was in 1588 we do not know, but wherever he was, he would have known, as in some sense most of his contemporaries would have known, that they had escaped disaster. I can recall similar feelings of people at the close of the weeks of the Battle of Britain. 1588 was a year of three eclipses, prognosticating doom, and the mightiest Armada ever launched was to come up the Channel to clinch the matter. There were Huguenots in London enough to tell what St Bartholomew's Eve had meant in France, and Walsingham's spies knew what Fifth Column work had been going on. And now the cloud was blown away:

> Incertainties now crown themselves assur'd
> And peace proclaims olives of endless age.
>
> Sonnet 107

No one supposed that it was the end of the matter, least of all a sensitive poet, but it gave him the opportunity to dramatize the situation, and he took it.

15

One might say that he made English history *visible* on the stage and *audible* in his plays. He used the language of gesture which involves people as liturgy does, gesture that comes before language, gesture that conveys the interplay of the many meanings of the words being used, the changing as well as the stable aspects. He begins to do this, awkwardly at first; but one day it will be near perfect. So Desdemona:

> I understand a fury in your words,
> But not the words.
>
> *Othello* IV.2.32–3

16

What he does in these plays is what Jacob Burckhardt nearly three centuries later meant by 'writing history is a poetic activity,' insisting that 'history finds in poetry not only its most important but also one of its finest sources.' Burckhardt was concerned primarily with what he called 'historical understanding', which sees that life is not a matter of ideas that can be synthesized in quiet contemplation but of choices that involve taking sides, choosing this and rejecting that. Donne's decision to become an Anglican is one such, Essex's attempt at rebellion is another, the Gunpowder Plot a third – and we might remember that Shakespeare knew personally at least half the conspirators. Historical understanding is an awareness of the choices that have to be made and of the danger that equivocation can end in a hideous death to those who come between 'the fell incensed points of mighty opposites'.

17

Poetic imagination in this business of arriving at essential history is very like our modern study of the movements of the great land masses on the surface of the earth. It feels like apparently solid earth moving, and it is full of foreboding. The great sequence of plays from *Richard II* to *Richard III* is a composite expression of that. It finds expression in prophecies, omens, and dreams, but deeper down in the motives, in the fears, in the choices that men and women make and the actual visible signs of the crumbling in the moral and spiritual fabric of society. So, you can have the blatant vigorous anti-papalism of the play *King John* (and not a word about Magna Carta) and the jingoism of

> Come the three corners of the world in arms
> And we shall shock them. Nought shall make
>   us rue
> If England to itself do rest but true,
>   *King John* v.vii.116–18

which is good copy for the *Daily Mail* and *Sun*.

But you can also have something which England at the end of the sixteenth century was very conscious of. Remember that Gresham founded the Royal Exchange in 1568.

> That smooth-faced gentleman, tickling commodity;
> Commodity, the bias of the world,
> The world, who of itself is peised well,
> Made to run even upon even ground,
> Till this advantage, this vile drawing bias,
> This sway of motion, this commodity,
> Makes it take head from all indifferency.
>   *King John* ii.i.573–9

That sounds very like suspicions of 'insider dealings'. The Queen's reign was ending in a gathering storm over monopolies, and under James I it would be more threatening. Remember, too, that Cromwell was born when *Hamlet* was being written, and young John Pym was an MP before the First Folio was published. The first quarter of the seventeenth century has been described as 'the period of greatest economic confusion in our history.'

18

What Shakespeare did was to read very carefully Holinshed's *Chronicles* (second edition 1587) and Hall and other sources, and having noted those twists and turns of choices made by kings and barons, to clothe in poetry the forces that were at work to break up the feudal structure, to foretell the new monarchy and the doctrine of the Divine Right of Kings, and to spell out the greater upheaval to come.

To take but one fragment, Holinshed wrote that in Parliament 'the Bishop of Carlisle, a man both learned, wise, and stout of stomach, boldlie showed forth his opinion concerning that demand, affirming that there was none among them willing and meet to give judgement upon so noble a prince as King Richard was, whom they had taken for sovereign and liege lord, by the space of two and twenty years and more,' and then recall Shakespeare's lines:

> Would God that any in this noble presence
> Were enough noble to be upright judge
> Of noble Richard. Then true noblesse would
> Learn him forbearance from so foul a wrong.
> What subject can give sentence on his king?
> And who sits here that is not Richard's subject?
> Thieves are not judged but they are by to hear,
> Although apparent guilt be seen in them;
> And shall the figure of God's majesty,
> His captain, steward, deputy elect,
> Anointed, crowned, planted many years,
> Be judged by subject and inferior breath,
> And he himself not present? ...
>   ... let me prophesy ...
> Disorder, horror, fear, and mutiny
> Shall here inhabit, and this land be called
> The field of Golgotha and dead men's skulls.
> O, if you rear this house against this house
> It will the woefullest division prove
> That ever fell upon this cursed earth!
> Prevent, resist it; let it not be so,
> Lest child, child's children, cry against you woe.
>   *Richard II* iv.i.108–20, 127, 133–40

'Wist ye not,' Elizabeth I is said to have observed, 'that I am Richard II?' It was but a generation later that we have a sad letter from Sir William Waller to his friend Sir Ralph Hopton as the Civil War began: 'The God of Peace in his good time send

us peace, and in the meantime fit us to receive it. We are both
on the stage, and we must act the parts that are assigned to us in
this tragedy.'

So whether we pause on the startling individualism of

> This word love which grey-beards call divine
> Be resident in men like one another,
> And not in me. I am myself alone,

or that long speech which was to come in *Troilus and Cressida*:

> Take but degree away, untune that string
> And hark what discord follows. Each thing meets
> In mere oppugnancy ...
> Then everything includes itself in power,
> Power into will, will into appetite;
> And appetite, an universal wolf,
> So doubly seconded with will and power,
> Must make perforce an universal prey
> And last eat up itself.
>
>   *Troilus and Cressida* I.iii.109–11, 119–24

There is fury in the words, and as Blackmur said: 'Language as
gesture creates meaning as conscience creates judgement, by feeling the pang, the inner bite of things forced together.' No one, I
think, looking at this twentieth century, can put this out of mind
unless he or she has reached a state of insensibility . Yeats said it:
'Mere anarchy is loosed upon the world.' Burckhardt, writing in
1846, said: 'None of you has any idea yet what a people is, and
how easily it deteriorates into a barbarous mob. You do not yet
know what a tyrannical rule is to be set up over the spirit.... We
may all perish, but I for one shall choose the cause for which I am
going to perish, the culture of old Europe.' And Unamuno said it
in our generation as Shakespeare had done, knowing that the
Divine Right of Kings has no solution to the problem.

19

I turn now to the Comedies of the early period. The gesture
here is the celebration of Romantic Love, something which had

been making its way into European culture since the twelfth century. Christendom had long celebrated Divine Love in the Mass, and it was in relation to that liturgical drama that the mystery plays developed, gained a degree of secular independence, and offered opportunities, as Renaissance culture gained ground, for this Romantic fiction to attract and gain popular attention.

Romantic Love asserts an exalted mode of living. It easily becomes foolish where it fails to engage those drawn into it in a relationship which can be both utterly self-giving and searchingly self-critical, an attitude to life which is neither utterly idealistic nor bitterly sceptical.

20

This celebratory playing, whether religious or secular, is the acting out of released imagination. It can play with all the elements of human behaviour from brutality to adoration. The games we play and the way we play them are indications of valued attitudes and conjectural explorations.

In the latter half of the sixteenth century, England had great numbers of travelling companies that brought such playing to all classes of people. The easiest forms of it were bawdy and farcical, and there is a considerable element of both in Shakespeare, though its language is not ours, and the 'greasiness', as it is called, is under control.

21

What it does do is to take the potentially most meaningful area of human life, that of sexual love, to play out the approaches to it in courtship, and up to marriage, the institution devised to contain it with some stability. What Shakespeare did in this field is, both in its early and later stages, of great significance. I have time only to refer to two plays of the first group: *As You Like It* and *Much Ado About Nothing*, both of which have great bearing on the spirituality expressed in Shakespeare's work.

22

Both plays are directly about love and marriage, light-heartedly playing with the themes and enabling the spiritual implications to find far-reaching expression. I am very conscious of feeling that not until Hardy's and Conrad's novels were written do we have the same kind of perception of what is involved. 'Pairing off', Conrad wrote, 'is the fate of mankind, and if two beings thrown together, mutually attracted, resist the necessity, fail in understanding, and voluntarily stop short of the embrace in the noblest meaning of that word, they are committing a sin against life, the call of which is simple, perhaps sacred.'

And again from Conrad: 'A young girl, you know, is something like a temple. You pass by and wonder what mysterious rites are going on there, what prayers and visions. The privileged man, the lover, the husband, who is given the key of the sanctuary, does not always know how to use it. For myself, without claim, without merit, simply by chance, I had been allowed to look through the half-opened door and I had seen the saddest possible desecration, the withered brightness of youth, a spirit neither made cringing nor yet dulled but as if bewildered in quivering hopelessness by gratuitous cruelty; self-confidence destroyed, and instead, a resigned recklessness, a mournful callousness (and all this simple, almost naive) before the material and moral difficulties of the situation.'

23

I bring these comments in because the Christian Church never doubted the importance of marriage (despite St Paul). It was both a secular reality that had to be 'christianized' and a sacrament to be received. But its handling of it was woeful. Dr Jack Dominian has said: 'Marriage has been the most impoverished of Christian experiences – and it is the most important.' Obviously there have been many factors contributing to this: the fear of sex, the subordination of women, the economic marketing to secure property; above all the lack of imagination in the evaluation of it, the failure to imagine the reality of it, that the love poetry of Donne and the dramatic poetry of Shakespeare were to assert.

> Eternity was in our lips and eyes,
> Bliss in our brows' bent; none our parts so poor
> But wase a race of heaven.
> > *Antony and Cleopatra* i.iii.35–7

This of course belongs to the love-tragedies, whereas it is the business of comedy to make its point by gentle mockery. No one was better able to do that than Rosalind.

> Love is merely a madness, and I tell you, deserves as well a dark house and a whip as madmen do; and the reason why they are not so punished and cured is that lunacy is so ordinary that the whippers are in love too.
> > *As You Like It* iii.iii.386–90

Love spins fantasies about men dying for it,

> But these are all lies. Men have died from time to time, and worms have eaten them, but not for love.
> > *As You Like It* iv.i.99–101

And it fantasizes about its permanence:

> Now tell me how long you would have her after you have possessed her?

And to Orlando's reply, 'For ever and a day,' she responds,

> Say a day without the ever. No, no Orlando; men are April when they woo, December when they wed. Maids are May when they are maids, but the sky changes when they are wives.
> > *As You Like It* iv.i.135–41

But Rosalind, besides being vulnerable because she herself is in love, brings to her arraignment of the young man the grace, charm, and imagination which is what Shakespeare was concerned to suggest was the woman's contribution to it – the essentially feminine awareness of the great range of human potentiality. At the time, because women did not actually play these parts, it had to be 'disguised', and this matter of how we employ fictions to express truth has its own questions to press for recognition.

24

Which takes me to *Much Ado About Nothing*, and to David Horowitz's book, *Shakespeare, an existential view* (1965), with the starting place this concept of Romantic Love. He speaks of it as Shakespeare turning to the springs of human grace and human creation, to the forces available 'for the repair of tragic ruin and for the renewal of human life.' Is that credible – Believest thou this? – when the notion of Romantic Love appears in such extravagant forms? Don Quixote for his Dulcinea? Horowitz argues: 'Of course there are absurdities but there is also a reality, and in its integrity, which it is our business to seek, there is that which is more than fiction, that which answers to an authentic experience transcending the mere physical action and decay.' 'Love is such a transcendence, it is the defining character of whatever human activity embodies what we call faith – not belief as such, not propositions, but what Buber always described as a "binding in relation", a trust in the other, a commitment to a relationship which approaches what must be called a "wholeness", transcending yet fulfilling the partners to it. This is the true nature of religion itself – or better put – of living religiously, and in this sense it is "quintessential Romance".'

25

The extravagance, the absurdity, the shallowness involved have all to be faced. In *Much Ado About Nothing* Shakespeare elects to have two pairs to play with, that of Claudio and Hero, and that of Benedick and Beatrice. The first of these, simply because it has little foundation beyond a man 'noting' a pretty girl, amounts to 'nothing' unless it can begin again after being jolted beyond mere appearances. The other begins at the level of scepticism:

> LEONATO Well, niece, I hope to see you one day
>   fitted with a husband.
> BEATRICE Not till God make men of some other
>   metal than earth. Would it not grieve a
>   woman to be over-mastered with a
>   piece of valiant dust?
>   *Much Ado About Nothing* II.i.51–5

And for Benedick, an equal measure of this scepticism:

> I will not be sworn but love may transform me to
> an oyster, but I'll take my oath on it, till he have
> made an oyster of me, she shall never make me
> such a fool. One woman is fair, yet I am well.
> Another is wise, yet I am well. Another virtuous,
> yet I am well. But till all graces be in one woman,
> one woman shall not come in my grace.
>   *Much Ado About Nothing* II.iii.23–9

26

Human beings are nevertheless open to revelation that such possibilities exist, to the incidence of a faith to engage oneself in such a relationship. The door is open to prove, albeit in costly fashion, at which comedy generally stops short, that human life is more than inconsequential dust, and other than either bestiality or nobility. Only by the acceptance of being drawn into such relationship does it become possible to get beyond 'appearances' to apprehend a truth which transcends mere noting.

27

So, the essence of Shakespearean love-comedy is religious perception. Lewis Mumford wrote: 'If religion be that which gives one a sense of things that are worth dying for, this community with all life, this central purpose in oneself inextricably bound

up with the nature of things, even those accidents and brutal
mischances that are so hard to assimilate, this faith may be called
a religion. For a good lover knows when to embrace, when to
conquer, and when to renounce, and he who loves life well will
not grudge the surrender or fail to recognize the appropriate
moment for it.'

He goes on to write that 'a marriage equally rich in every season is an exception. If people realized this more, they might face
bad periods more cheerfully and be more patient.'

The shift of the novel from the approach to marriage to what
happens later has been one of the most significant steps taken by
fiction to look at this. What Shakespeare did in these comedies
was to make clear the starting off point.

Edwin Muir would say,

> Yet still from Eden springs the root
> As clean as on the starting day ...
>   'One Foot in Eden'

and I think Browning put something of it into a woman's mouth
in answering the charge that she had misconceived it all:

> O love, no, love, not so indeed
> You were just weak earth, I knew
> With much in you waste, and many a weed
> And plenty of passions run to seed
> But a little good grain too.
>
> And such as you were, I took you for mine:
> Did you not find me yours?
> To wait the olive and watch the vine
> And wonder when rivers of oil and wine
> Would flow as the book assures.
>
> Well, and if none of those good things came
> What did the failure prove?
> The man was my whole world just the same
> With his flowers to praise and his weeds to blame
> And either or both to love.

You may reject this, even mock it, but Shakespeare, as I will try
to say later in coming to the last plays, suggests that the
transfiguration implies also things like healing, redemption, and
salvation or wholeness.

28

It means also facing the experience of the Tragedies, where, as in
prayer, we come to silence beyond words. Death releases the
player and 'since no man has aught of what he leaves, what
isn't to leave betimes?' (*Hamlet* v.ii.168–70). Let be. 'The rest is
silence' (*Hamlet* V.2.310). I can only look briefly at one or two of
these plays and consider what is distinctively Shakespearean in
them.

29

It was something which Nikolaus Pevsner, in his book *The
Englishness of English Art*, drew attention to years ago. Quoting a
line from *Romeo and Juliet* (III.v.2),

It was the nightingale and not the lark,

he wondered how that would have been said in German or
Italian; and George Steiner, in *After Babel*, comments: 'Shakespeare's stance on language is a calm tenancy, an at homeness in
a sphere of expressive, executive means whose roots, traditional
strengths and tonalities, as yet unexploited riches, he recognized
as a man's hand will recognize the struts and cornices, the worn
places and the new, in his father's house.' Pevsner said: 'There is
a spirit of an age and there is a natural character that takes hold
of all that it has inherited from the past or wider world, and
shapes it, sometimes clumsily, sometimes superbly, to make an
English version of what it values in them.'

Pevsner had no doubt that though Shakespeare could burst
the categories into which one might try to force him, he was
indisputably English, the Englishman who keeps long silences
and when he speaks does so in a low voice, as Hamlet himself
required:

> ... in the very torrent, tempest and I may say the
> whirlwind of your passion, you must acquire
> and beget a temperance that may give it
> smoothness ... with this special observance, that
> you o'erstep not the modesty of nature ... (nor)
> make the judicious grieve.
>
> *Hamlet* III.ii.6–8, 18–19, 26

It is a spirit described by another writer as 'reverence for
moral music', and its tradition includes the Authorized Version
of the Bible, Hooker and Andrewes, Bunyan and Traherne. 'It
does not tear a passion to tatters so much as contain it.' One
may see it in Macduff's reaction to the news of the death of his
children:

> All my pretty ones
> Did you say all?
>
> *Macbeth* IV.iii.217–18

and in Othello's

> But yet the pity of it, Iago. O, Iago, the pity of it,
> Iago!
>
> *Othello* IV.i.191–2

and in *Hamlet*, in the words of the dying Laertes:

> Exchange forgiveness with me, noble Hamlet.
> Mine and my father's death come not upon thee,
> Nor thine on me.
>
> *Hamlet* v.ii.281–3

30

To continue with Hamlet. Many years ago T. S. Eliot described
the play as, 'far from being Shakespeare's masterpiece, it is most
certainly an artistic failure.' Reading this as an undergraduate in
1925 I was very impressed. Sixty years later I think the comment
is much more certainly one of Eliot's too-clever-by-half mis-
judgements, from a perversity that was deep in his nature. He

argued that Hamlet (the man) was dominated by an emotion which is inexpressible because it is in excess of the facts as they appear. 'Hamlet's bafflement at the absence of an objective equivalent to his feelings is a prolongation of the bafflement of his creator in the face of his artistic problem.' I should say that the facts were so painfully recognized by Hamlet that he hovered between feigned and real madness in facing them.

> How stand I then
> That have a father killed, a mother stained,
> Excitement of my reason and my blood?
> *Hamlet* iv.iv.47–9

Add to that the whole court, with Ophelia, Polonius, Rosencrantz and Guildenstern, involved in the evil corruption, in a villainy too horrible to contemplate, dishonesty like a fog surrounding them all. How can words hold it or actions deal with it? Only after his return from the ship where he has sent Rosencrantz and Guildenstern to their death, does he take the line of swift action. Evil is not a problem to be solved. It is to be endured, out-lived.

> The readiness is all.
> *Hamlet* v.ii.168

In his heart there remains a kind of fighting that will not let him sleep and he acts without cynicism or resignation or bluster to go to his death:

> If it be now, 'tis not to come. If it be not come,
> it will be now: If it be not now, yet it will come.
> *Hamlet* v.ii.166–8

It is the power of acceptance that is his spiritual strength.

31

But we must not be so hooked onto character problems as to lose sight of the society and its institutions in which human lives are interwoven. The Tragedies, for the most part, are set in royal courts, in princely circles; Elizabethan England knew enough of

Machiavelli's treatise and the jockeying for political power that never halted, to recognize what was at stake, not just for the leading personages, but for all those who were drawn along by or into their purposes:

> I see
> The imminent death of twenty thousand men
> That for a fantasy and trick of fame
> Go to their graves like beds; fight for a plot
> Wherein the numbers cannot try the cause
> Which is not tomb enough and continent
> To hide the slain.
>
> *Hamlet* IV.iv.59–65

We now know that there is a rate of inflation in these things, so that a Napoleonic quip. 'What's a million men?' will mark the progress to our own times. And we can contemplate the many millions …

And it follows hard upon that dissolution of the social bonds which in *King Lear* is noted:

> Love cools, friendship falls off, brothers divide; in cities mutinies; in countries discord; in palaces treason; and the bond cracked 'twixt son and father…. The King falls from bias of nature; there's father against child.
>
> *King Lear* I.ii.104–7, 108–9

Or as Donne put it:

> 'Tis all pieces, all coherence gone;
> All just supply and all Relation,
> Prince, Subject, Father, Sonne, all things forgot
> For every man alone thinks he has got
> To be a Phoenix.
>
> 'An Anatomie of the World'

If there is no such thing as society, what else do you expect?

King Lear presents a wide range of opinion about the human condition and the forces that governed it, from zodiacal to divine malignant sport,

as if we were villains on necessity, fools by heavenly compulsion, knaves, thieves and treachers
by spherical predominance, drunkards, liars,
and adulterers by an enforced obedience of
planetary influence.

King Lear I.ii.119–23

or as if, we were flies to the gods or merely the victims of our
own wilfulness.

It reflected the seething London theatre where Marlowe had
preached irreligion, telling men not to be afraid of bugbears or
hobgoblins, till he ended his career in that tavern brawl of
secret agents in 1593 and his *Elegies* were burned publicly in
1599. Men and women were forced to be conscious of the slip-
pery nature of their footholds in such a society, and indeed in
the cosmos itself. Shakespeare was born in the same year as
Galileo, and knew that 'conscience' – consciousness – made
cowards of men and played on their fears. So Cardinal Wolsey
takes his farewell:

This is the state of man: today he puts forth
The tender leaves of hopes; tomorrow blossoms,
And bears his blushing honours thick on him;
The third day comes a frost, a killing frost,
And when he thinks, good easy man, fully surely
His greatness is a-ripening, nips his root,
And then he falls as I do ...
And when he falls, he falls like Lucifer,
Never to hope again.

King Henry VIII, III.ii.353–9, 372–3

32

Some years ago the Bishop of Liverpool published a little
book, called *Bias to the Poor*, a plea that there was a Christian
obligation to act on behalf of the poor. It was not exactly a
novel theme in English history, but it excited hostility, as did
also *Faith in the City* and Peter Townsend's work. The critics did

not exactly fall back on Elizabethan orders to whip the rogues
but there was resentment that an issue should be made of this
poverty.

It is not the main factor in *King Lear*, but it comes into view in
Act 3 when Lear begins to go mad, his royal dignity destroyed,
his world turned upside down.

> Art cold?
> I'm cold myself. – Where is this straw, my fellow?
> The art of our necessities is strange,
> And can make vile things precious. Come, your
>   hovel.
>
> *King Lear* iii.ii.68–71

Lear is by this time stripped of every vestige of power, bereft
of all relationships, save those who are thrust out of society like
himself, and it is from the margin of society that the comment
comes:

> The usurer hangs the cozener.
> Through tatter'd clothes great vices do appear;
> Robes and furred gowns hide all. Plate sin with
>   gold,
> And the strong lance of justice hurtless breaks;
> Arm it in rags, a pygmy's straw doth pierce it.
>   ... Get thee glass eyes
> And, like a scurvy politician, seem
> To see the things thou dost not.
>
> *King Lear* iv.v.159–63, 166–8

When Lear realizes that this is what he had never seen till he
himself was cast out,

> O, I have ta'en
> Too little care of this,
>
> *King Lear* iii.iv.33–4

he puts all social relationships under judgement.

Elsewhere another incident takes place. A nameless servant
interferes in the blinding of Gloucester and kills the Duke of
Cornwall.

A peasant stand up thus!

King Lear iii.vii.78

exclaims Reagan. Something has brought a change, and though
it cannot divert the course of tragedy it is a note of humanity
deeper than the social distinctions. Even Edmund can be
touched to act in a new way.

Some good I mean to do,
Despite of mine own nature.

King Lear v.ii.218–19

Lear, Cordelia, the Fool, the peasant, and Gloucester are dead,
but in the experience of this tragedy

You have seen
Sunshine and rain at once, her smiles and tears
Were like a better way.

King Lear iv.iii.17–19

At least we have a chance to see it.

33

One of the gifts of the Spirit, as John understood things, is this:
'He will declare to you the things that are to come' (John 16.13).
And there will be in all great art and literature a certain prophetic
insight, not in the time-space dimension so much as in the quali-
tative presence and relationship of human beings: the things
which human society must needs face and in which our emphasis
upon love-binding-in-relation men and women will be tested. We
shall be required to grow up to greater spiritual maturity.

34

One of the things to come gained dramatic expression about
1604 in *Othello*. We now live very near to its storm centres. In
1600 the good ship *Eagle* brought to London the Moorish
embassy. It was a business and political affair. They stayed on for
several months and it was generally felt to be an outrage to the

susceptibilities of Londoners. No one could have foreseen the centuries of white imperialist expansion, of genocide, of slave-trading, of immigration of coloured peoples, and the conse-quences of these things. We cannot treat the play *Othello* simply as character conflict. That is there within the wider context, where cultural deficiencies and flaws are to be met.

35

Let us take a word from one black artist about it: Paul Robeson insisted, 'Shakespeare meant Othello to be a black moor from Africa,' the colour as a culture shock, as it still remains for millions, a spark that can ignite fears and hatred in any number of localities. You may recall some of the comments made in the play. To Rodrego, Othello is 'an extravagant and wheeling stranger' (*Othello* 1.i.138), like a malign comet that has entered our atmosphere. So whereas Othello and Desdemona respond to the specifically personal sexual way of loving, Iago is able to sub-merge that response in a collective intolerance and hatred. He typifies Othello as an animal, as the Nazis spoke of Jews as ver-min. The real thrust of the play is the implication that the audi-ence disliked the Moor, that there is that in all of us. Culturally conditioned, that can give genocide its head. It is not a black man but a Sioux Indian who says that the way white men think about the world leads inevitably to the violation of the earth and humanity. We might well reflect on such genocide on a conti-nental scale.

And in this play, as in that of Calvary, women are the wit-nesses to the tragedy that ensues.

36

Macbeth brings the matter nearer home, to these fair islands, but from the outset we are warned of a world which reverses all humane values:

> Fair is foul, and foul is fair,
> Hover through the fog and filthy air.
> *Macbeth* 1.i.10–11

No play has quite so much darkness in it, nor such concentrations on disease and bloodshed. The implication is that it is not the good angels who keep their ancient places, but that if you 'turn a stone and start a wing', it will be the whole brood of devils and evil spirits you will meet. Ask yourself briefly the next time you read or see *Macbeth* what evidence of a world redeemed is permitted. What it deals with is rather a universe such as Paracelsus pictured. This work was almost immediately available in England at the end of the sixteenth century, where man shares the universe with a vast army of evil creatures, the brood of chaos and old night, creatures that lie in wait for men and women to seduce them to murder and damnation. Paracelsus taught that this world of devils was everywhere present, a world permanently dark and infested by evil. Disease, like the plague that constantly swept through cities, was but one token of it, witchcraft and murder others. The porter of Macbeth's castle is jocularly and veritably a porter at Hell's gate. What we need to remember is that though there were efforts to stem the tide of crazy demonology, Trevor-Roper rightly reminds us that in Europe as a whole the period 1600–50 was worse than the two half centuries preceding it. By that latter date some nine million people had burned to death since 1484. What is enacted in *Macbeth* is damnation with a terrible question to face:

> Did Heaven look on
> And would not take their part?
>   Macbeth iv.iii.223–4

37

But that wasn't Shakespeare's last word on the play to be played out. We have four plays – *Pericles*, *Cymbeline*, *The Winter's Tale*, and *The Tempest* to reflect on of a different character, plays not always popular today. They may have been his way of coping with changing taste, with changed theatre conditions, a deliberate lightening of the playing with 'spirits' and storms, and in particular a lengthening of the time factor: twelve to twenty years in *The Tempest* and *Cymbeline*, sixteen years in *The Winter's Tale* and possibly longer in *Pericles*.

38

What the extension of time makes possible is something which we attach to words like patience, endurance, long-suffering, grace, hope, fulfilment, redemption, resurrection. There is the finding of that which had been lost, the restoration of things which had gone awry or suffered shipwreck. These things have closely to do with living to maturity, to ripeness, to meaningfulness, which depends upon grasping the significance of extended experience. The wrong and blind choices, the prodigal wickedness of one generation or person may be redeemed, enduring love may be crowned, constancy vindicated.

39

This is not simply like shuffling the cards for a better deal. Instead it lives out the hope of something that 'rights the disasters' that have been experienced. It looks forward, as Prospero says:

> Let us not burden our remembrance with
> A heaviness that's gone,
>
> *The Tempest* v.i.202–3

but it does not propose to try to forget the past – rather to utilize memory as an important factor in the spiritual life. It is not rightly used if it is simply a looking backwards, a trying to live in the past:

> Only one youth, and the bright life was shrouded,
> Only one morning, and the day was clouded,
> And one old age with all regrets is crowded.

On the contrary the right use of memory is that it affords us the opportunity to use the vastness of that which qualitatively we have been immersed in, something far more important than a vast space. With it,

> Love talks with better knowledge,
> Knowledge with dearer love.
>
> *Measure for Measure* iii.ii.163–4

Where there can be shared recognition of this, which is what religious celebration is about – absolution and restoration – you have what is adumbrated in *Titus Andronicus* (v.iii.70–2):

> O let me teach you how to knit again
> This scattered corn into one mutual sheaf
> These broken limbs into one body

and echoes the prayer for Eucharist in the Didache.
It gains full expression in *The Winter's Tale* (v.ii.14–16):

> They looked as if they had heard of a world
> ransomed, or one destroyed. A notable passion
> of wonder appeared in them ...

It is time to awake out of sleep, to see things made new, and to greet them. It may be Ferdinand's

> Oh, you wonder!
>
> *The Tempest* i.ii.428

or Miranda's

> O wonder!
> How many goodly creatures there are here.
> How beauteous mankind is! O brave new world
> That has such people i'nt.
>
> *The Tempest* v.i.184–7

The storms are real enough, the cruelties, the pains and agonies are hideous, but they make way for the music of the spheres, and patience is the guide to this ransomed world.

And Shakespeare chose four young girls, Marina, Imogen, Perdita and Miranda, to be the bearers of that hope. One may deny the ability of poetry to express this sense of a transcendent reality, which it is certainly the business of religion to afford us, but the greatest of the poets of Christendom thought otherwise, and Dante remembered the young girl Beatrice through all his stormy life and all his contemplation of human experience.

C. Day Lewis has it in his poem *The Album*:

> Then I see her, petalled in new-blown hours,
> Beside me – 'All you love most there
> Has blossomed again,' she murmurs, 'all that
>   you missed there
> Has grown to be yours.'

As Prospero says, in conclusion,

> But release me from my bands
> With the help of your good hands ...
> And my ending is despair
> Unless I be relieved by prayer.
>   *The Tempest* v.i.9–10, 15–16

And a line out of *Love's Labour's Lost* (v.ii.632) must be always kept in mind,

> This is not generous, not gentle, not humble,

a reminder that the greatest of the twelve moral virtues is magnanimity.

And gentle Shakespeare was the poet of such magnanimity.

14

ON EDVARD MUNCH'S
PAINTING THE SCREAM

Later he started talking about suffering as if that
were some sort of universal language. It's certainly a universal condition, something like what
you called the murmur of contingency – as if
the planet, talking to itself, cries out and com-
plains. Perhaps when distant people on the
planets pick up some wavelengths of ours, all
they hear is a continuous scream.

IRIS MURDOCH *The Message to the Planet*

One great big scream, come from no one knows
where … one's soul perhaps … I'm certain that
death, real death, is just that scream, rising,
rising, till-flick-it shrivels up, the very last bit of
silence. No silence in the next world, eh Philip?

G. BERNANOS *Monsieur Quine*

I sank down to the bottom of that scream, like a
capsized boat

ibid

In 1893, the Norwegian painter Edvard Munch completed the
first version of his picture known as *The Scream* or *The Cry*. He
had written in his diary of the previous year, 'I looked at the
flaming clouds that hung like blood and a sword over the blue-
black fjord and city. I stood there trembling with fright. And I
felt a loud unending scream piercing nature.' Munch returned
to this theme many times during the following years. He wrote

frequently of its sharp, arresting presence in his mind. Perhaps to the very end of his life he felt himself to be trapped in that nightmare world where the scream is frozen into a voiceless terror.

The picture itself has good claims to be regarded as one of the most significant pictures of the modern world, and a recent study of it by Reinhold Heller (*Art in Context*, The Penguin Press) helps to illuminate its importance for us today. The great strides made since the picture was painted in the fields of psychology, psychoanalysis, cultural anthropology and alienation have made it an object of far greater interest than it could have possibly been before. We have learned to see that great pictures, like great plays, novels and poems, are expressions of much more than the so-called experience of the painter or poet or novelist, or we have changed our understanding of how a poet or painter does experience things at all. Such men and women draw into themselves the much wider currents of the seething tempestuous world in which they are present. They record like the most delicate seismographs the shocks and tremors that occur and pass unregarded by others. The agonies and pains of travailing Creation gain from them formal expression through the imaginative grasp of such material and events that constitutes the artistic power of the man or woman at work. They are 'open to the world' in a way and to a degree that others are not: they are related to it by ties that involve them in its pangs. In this sense, every great work of art and literature is a cry or scream.

Munch's picture then can be compared with novels by Dostoievsky or Kafka, with poems like *The Waste Land*, with a play like *Waiting for Godot*. We cannot easily forget Mishkin's scream at the moments of illumination nor 'the agony in stony places'. Nor can we fail to see how Picasso's *Guernica* brings the screaming into our own day, though Munch's picture had far wider connotations. He himself wrote of it, 'I felt the great scream through Nature,' and added still more ominously, 'Only someone insane could paint like this.' Year by year he returned to it later, repeating these words, as if he himself were nailed to the suffering body of Nature, as if he himself could do no other than continue to cry out.

Out of these depths, what shamefaced cry
Half choked in the dry throat, as though a stone
Were our confounded tongue, can ever rise:
Because the mind has been struck blind
And may no more conceive
The throne ...

DAVID GASCOYNE

In these days, when we speak much of symbols and cast about
to discover how we may tell what is real to others, we can learn
much from Munch's picture.

Our present purpose is to take notice of it in its bearing upon
our spirituality, upon the way in which we endeavour to relate
our lives to ultimate concern. It is a field in which crying out is
not uncommon. Men and women have cried out to the Lord in
their distress throughout the centuries. They have cried out as
watchmen, as prophets, as prisoners. 'And about the ninth hour
Jesus cried out with a loud voice,' and sometimes we hear that
crying even now.

What is that sound high in the air
Murmur of maternal lamentation ...

A sound of weeping over a doomed city should not be difficult
to hear, if only our ears could be unstopped. Perhaps we have
grown too used to reading the words with our eyes alone to catch
or be caught by the peculiar pains that shaped their cries. 'A
voice crying in the wilderness' doesn't easily disturb us because
we don't conceive of our civilized world as such. We have no
lively expectation that the stones by the wayside will cry out to
anyone sensitive enough to hear them. If they cry out to God, it
might even be embarrassing to overhear what they had to say.
The cry of Nature, it must be admitted, has in our own day
become too shrill to be ignored completely. Perhaps the first
steps towards new life can only come when incessant crying per-
mits us to sleep no more.

Our Hebrew-Christian spirituality is bound up inextricably
with such crying out. It may well be that above all else we need
to take note of this and make our return to the wellsprings of its

truth. Perhaps we are too ashamed as yet to confess the extremity of our needs. But Munch's picture once truly 'seen'

> would, if it were cold
> And in the icy silence of the tomb,
> So haunt thy days and chill thy dreaming nights

that it could enable us to begin to hear the cry that now goes up from our world.

It could do no more than this. It could send us back to the foundations of our spirituality to observe that the great departure or exodus points come when the cries are made. 'Their cry came up unto God by reason of their bondage.' 'Behold, the cry of the children of Israel is come unto me. I am come to deliver them.' The cries of the oppressed are heard and God moves in reply to them.

Is it so still or has God changed his ways? Do we even know what it means to cry out to God in the expectation that he will act? Do we range ourselves along with those who have reason to cry out both day and night, whose throats are weary with crying? This Hebrew faith was no easy short-term matter then, nor can it ever be, but it clung through all the centuries to the faith that the cry is heard. It was ground out with infinite pain between the millstones of apparently fortuitous and retributive suffering. It required the faithful, in Bernard Malamud's phrase, 'to put on suffering like an overcoat.'

'There are times of suffering,' writes Iris Murdoch in *The Black Prince*, 'which remain in our lives like black absolutes and are not blotted out. Fortunate are those for whom these black stars shed some sort of light.' As long as human history endures, the black absolutes are going to keep their places: so long must the cry of the oppressed go up. So long too must it be a matter of spiritual health to have ears to hear, though the price to be paid will be an end for ever to our sleep. It is characteristic of much modern American novel-writing that it prompts, and turns back again and again, to the question, 'Who doth hear?' Kafka assured us long ago that the inmates of the Penal Colony ('Denmark's a prison ...') would be ingeniously silenced, and there can be little doubt that the lesson has been learned. Is crying then, outmoded for ever?

What is there to cry about? Our greatest difficulty is that kind of obtuseness, of being enclosed in our own fat, which makes it hard to perceive the pains and pangs of the processes of new birth. Those of us who inhabit a world grown old in its ways and insured against all conceivable disasters may be more inclined to note our own discomforts than the travails of newcomers to the scene. Our so-called spirituality may be much more self-regarding than we have learned to admit. Preoccupied with our own survival, we may be quite incapable of seeing that the great issues of the contemporary scene have already bypassed our intentions. The first and vital step towards reality in living is to become aware of the cries of those whose supplications made in the darkness of the black absolutes have entered into the ears of the Lord God.

To take such a step at all must require of the sophisticated world a movement of the spirit that strikes a retrogressive note almost barbaric in nature. We are likely to be offended, for example, by the manners of the oppressed. An Eldridge Cleaver, a Malcolm X, a Paulo Freire, to say nothing of the raucous voices in our own society, can hardly help offending. 'To your tents, O Israel' sounds discouraging to those who thought they were getting somewhere. 'This people that knoweth not the Law,' uncouth and raw and violent, this scum of the world that threatens to pour out of its shanty towns and tenements to defile our 'peaceful' streets like a horde of rats, is not easily perceived to be that poor whom none but the Living God has regarded. To say that we must go back to the tents of Israel to be reborn as possible dwellers in the world now being shaped by other hands than ours must sound grotesque. To imply that the God in whose Name we have done many mighty works may require such things of us must sound offensive if not ludicrous. A God of such originality must prove to be too awkward for our ways. We find it hard to believe that such a drastic metanoia is called for. Apocalyptic is all very well at the distance of well-nigh two millennia. Munch and his blood-red clouds and his screaming Nature we would prefer to set aside.

Yet the great title-deeds of our faith continue to remind us of

these cries that we fail to hear. They continue to suggest that a
return to a point where the cries can be heard is a necessary step
for God's people to take. Not for nothing has the God of Israel
invited his servants to participate in his work in the world. By no
stretch of imagination can it be supposed that, like idle appren-
tices, they can ignore what the craftsman himself has planned.
Return, return, return, means in our modern idiom, relearn,
relearn, relearn. A new kind of consciousness is called for. A new
kind of relationship must be shaped. A new mode of understanding must be fashioned. 'Ye have not passed this way heretofore' and the ground is difficult to master. The extent of the
suffering we have hardly begun to fathom, but this God will have
us participate in it along with himself. Those who do not appreciate this can hardly be said to be with us now.

To say this is not to despise or to lose sight of the work of the
past. It is not even a matter now of judging whether the mission
of the Church to the Graeco-Roman world was carried out well
or ill. That task, that world, that spirituality forged for the task,
belong to the past. A new world has risen upon us, a new consciousness must take possession of it. What then have we to take
with us as we offer ourselves to be re-enlisted in that continuing
mission? Most of all, it would seem, we take the faith that we
have to do with the God who hears the cries of his people. We
have to hear them too for they are the necessary antecedents of
a genuine grasp of a theology of Hope or an Exodus theology
such as we talk of today. Sebastian Moore was so right in saying:
'What is it that all the scholars lack? It is the unremitting pressure of the human situation on Jesus.... He saw himself defined
by the situation.' Extend that remark to an awareness of the
pressure of circumstances now, and what can we do but become
hearers of the Cry? With the Cry in our ears an Exodus theology is a living response; without such hearing it can be only an
interesting exercise. The painful travail of our own rebirth
begins when we are caught up in that cry, when once again we
ourselves 'have no language but a cry'.

15

ON WILLIAM MORRIS

When invited to come and speak as a Christian Socialist, I was eager to talk about William Morris for a number of reasons. Most importantly it is vital that those who have their roots in Christian Socialism should gird themselves afresh to another round of the struggle while they have yet time, in order to face as boldly as possible what has to be done in Britain in these years. The Socialist movement has never faced at such depth hitherto the task of renewing and recreating its forces to engage with the anti-democratic, inhuman, wasteful, contemptuous and secrecy-delighting regime which has gone far in ten years to destroy much that a responsible and humane policy had endeavoured to create in Britain. Our task is not just to win elections, but to renew foundations, recover vision, deepen conviction, and so in time be able to re-establish the democratic institutions set up to act for the great purpose of giving healthy and meaningful life to every man, woman and child.

I say renew because that purpose has deep roots in British history, as in other parts of the world where men and women have struggled for justice and freedom. In British history comes the faith of John Ball and the Peasants, so beloved of Morris, the faith of the Levellers and Diggers in the seventeenth century, the purpose of those who founded the early Unions in the eighteenth century, and the determination of the Chartists and Socialists of the last century.

Christian Socialism has a place for ideas, theological, political, and sociological, but first and foremost it is concerned with human beings and society as a fellowship of such people. We do well to learn from those now in the thick of the struggle, and those before them who behaved bravely. I count William Morris one to be honoured for his spirit and achievements. Among

other things he did Morris wrote songs for Socialists, and hymns.
In the parish church of my childhood in the Potteries we sang:

> Hear a word, a word in season,
> For the day is drawing nigh
> When the cause shall call upon us
> Some to live and some to die.
>
> He that dies shall not die lonely,
> Many a one hath gone before,
> He that lives shall bear no burden
> Heavier than the life they bore.

The cause itself is fundamentally about recovering and learning
to live by a deep sense of shared life, overcoming the things that
divide us, learning, as Morris said, 'to face our fellows and speak
out whatever really burns inside us', and proving in actual living
that all who have ever lived in this cause live in us, as Edwin
Muir put it:

> The dead in their silence keep me in memory,
> Have me in hold. To all I am bounden.

So it is in the spiritual strength of the great company of
named and nameless men and women we go about our lives.
This truth was expressed by the way a Lancashire Branch of the
SDF received the news of Morris's death: 'Comrade Morris is
not dead. There is not a Socialist living would believe him dead,
for he lives in the heart of all true men and women still, and will
do so to the end of time.'

William Morris was unusually gifted, but also fortunate. Being
born well-to-do he had a good education and was able to spend
his life as he chose. But he did not escape hardship and calamities.
His marriage became a sad affair, and his relations with many
Socialists were strained. He was able, however, to hold his course
of giving what he had in him to the thing he came so passionately
to believe in: the common life, or Commonwealth as he called it.
He learned to do this inwardly as well as outwardly, something
which Carl Jung has described as 'doing something real for the
world, shouldering an infinitesimal part of the gigantic unsolved

problems of our day.' Commonwealth meant something to him
which I suspect lies behind those two brief descriptions of the first
generation of Christians in the Acts of the Apostles, 'All that
believed were together' and 'they held all things in common'.

Morris was also a poet. We are told that when he went to
Oxford in 1853 all the young men talked poetry and it was the
poetry of Tennyson that bewitched them; for many of them no
doubt a land of refuge from the harsh realities of the age of
Palmerston, the Crimean War, the disputes over Darwinism and
Christian beliefs, and the chill philosophy of Self-Help. Some of
them like Matthew Arnold listened to the melancholy long withdrawing roar of the sea of faith and stood their ground,

> Wandering between two worlds, one dead,
> The other powerless to be born;
> With nowhere yet to rest my head
> Like these on earth I wait forlorn.
> 'Stanzas from La Grande Chartreuse'

But the majority of Tennysonians tended to weave tapestries of
words on the Arthurian legends and medieval stories of courtly
love, picturesque poetizing which with the pre-Raphaelites produced a studio view of life with an atmosphere of incense.

Morris, I think, was saved from the worst features of such
romanticizing by an architectural understanding and genuine
countryside passion; he really knew what fourteenth-century
churches were like, and could imagine the unspoiled countryside. Furthermore Chaucer gave him a stable foundation to
offset the dreamier passions of the medievalists. So, though
there is in him a good deal of making a religion of poetry, it was
saved from being an escape from reality by a genuine appreciation of the craftsman's and mason's work in the Middle Ages. It
was not sham Gothicism as so much of contemporary work
tended to be. So the big work – the Collected Poems called *The
Earthly Paradise* – was genuine because Morris did see the countryside as a scene of paradisal beauty. Yeats was right when he said
that Morris was not one of the great poets, but one of the happi-
est; and he was happy about real things. Because he genuinely
loved the Epping Forest of his childhood, and the Thames

Valley and its villages, he did not lose touch with the reality of
human experience. He rejoiced in Icelandic sagas and tales of
classical Greece, but he was at his best when he came home to
his bit of the Earthly Paradise:

> Forget six counties with smoke,
> Forget the snorting steam and piston stroke,
> Forget the spreading of the hideous town,
> Think rather of the pack horse on the down,
> And dream of London small and white and clean,
> The clear Thames bordered by her gardens green.

We know that fourteenth-century London was anything but
clean, even if an unpolluted Thames ran through it. The plague
ravaged it every generation and the great majority of people
lived short and hard lives; but their villages and churches had
much beauty in them. An element in Morris's poetry has that
quality too:

> O Love, turn from the unchanging sea, and gaze
> Down these grey slopes upon the year grown old,
> A-dying mid the autumn-scented haze,
> That rangeth o'er the hollow in the wold,
> Where the wind-bitten ancient elms enfold
> Grey church, long barn, orchard and red-roofed stead,
> Wrought in dead days for men a long while dead.

> Come down, O love, may not our hands still meet
> Since still we live today, forgetting June,
> Forgetting May, deeming October sweet –
> O hearken, hearken, through the afternoon
> The grey tower sings a strange old tinkling tune,
> Sweet, sweet and sad, the toiling year's last breath,
> Too satiate of life to strive with death.

No doubt it was the 'passion of the past' as Tennyson called it,
but it was a genuine passion – intense to the point of death – and
if it was often overtaken by a sense of anguish, that too was
authentic, and bravely acknowledged.

Morris was also an artist and craftsman of an astonishing

imaginative breadth and versatility. There was scarcely a craft
that he did not do extremely well, weaving, dyeing cloth, making
pottery and tiles, stained glass, furniture and wallpapers. He was
also a businessman, a leading member of the firm Morris,
Marshall, Faulkner and Co., founded in 1861 with capital of
£100 loaned by Morris's mother. It was to continue until 1940.
Its productions attracted attention, even imitators, so that its
main influence in the domestic field was something of a revolution in taste. Morris was not a great innovator in the arts, as has
sometimes been claimed, because many of the great changes in
design for wallpapers, carpets and textiles had already occurred
in the decade before this with pioneers like Owen Jones, but
Morris did exercise enormous influence by the sheer beauty of
his designs and the quality of workmanship.

As important as this was his understanding of the worker and
work in the field of art. As intensely as Ruskin, he believed that
any art should express the moral being and sense of pleasure in
creativity of a man in his work. 'What I mean by art', he said, 'is
some creation which appeals to the emotions and intellect of the
worker.' He was insistent that all artistic production be seen therefore in terms of its impact and influence upon the society for
which it was produced as well as in its design and in the conditions
it was made.

It did not escape him that most of the productions of his firm
went to embellish the homes of well-to-do people while the great
mass of the population continued to live in ugly squalid conditions, and were employed in days of labour which were anything
but pleasurable and in many cases exhausting and unhealthy.
Increasingly it drove him to face the question of how such an outrage of the very nature of art and of the lives of human beings
could be rejected and replaced by a way of life which fulfilled
rather than destroyed human nature. It is a question that is still
with us: the creativity of men and women has been extended far
further without fundamentally changing the relationships within
society. Whenever I come up to London I try to go to the Whitechapel Art Gallery – not only as it has most striking exhibitions
but also it presses the question home, 'What have these works of
art got to do with and for the Whitechapel Road outside?'

The way of answering Morris's self-questioning came, I think, by way of his sense of history. To begin with it allowed him to romanticize the medieval world, but it also gave him, because he never lost his craftsman's sense of touching materials, the basis for what may be called 'historical materialism', so that when he began to read Marx and Engels it was not theories of surplus value and philosophical materialism that gripped him, but the historical analysis that portrayed the nature of the social changes that had brought into being the capitalist world. There was in 1880 very little literature available to help him but with a few clues he began to see daylight. He looked squarely at the conditions of life for the masses of people around him and decided 'if civilization is to go no further than this, it had better not have gone so far; if it does not aim at getting rid of this misery, and giving some share of happiness and dignity of life to all people that it has created, it is simply an organized injustice, a mere instrument of oppression, so much the worse than that which has gone before it, as its pretensions are higher, its slavery subtler, its mastery harder to overthrow.'

This means history is meaningless, or a mere pastime, unless it compels and helps us to look critically at the relationships which obtain in the structure of society to which we belong. Without such a sense of history it is easy to turn a blind eye to the cost of it all in human terms. To adapt a phrase of Tom Paine's, one could praise beautiful plumage and forget the dying bird.

Over in France this year they are celebrating the two hundredth anniversary of the French Revolution. Just what major reflections will emerge it is too soon to say, but it is worth noting that Catholic historians have stopped denouncing the satanic character of the Revolution and begun to look at society in a different fashion, and consider the gains through looking at society now.

What we should ask, I think, is how British society, then and later, could be so cruel to the poorest and weakest. How could it be civilized when in the mill-towns and the Potteries women and children could be treated with such cruelty? In the Potteries during the 1830s children of five years and upwards worked from

6 a.m. to 8 p.m. six days a week for a shilling. In the cotton mills hordes of children were beaten to keep them awake. In Whitehaven Cemetery there is still a stone recording the names of scores of children aged eight and upwards who were killed in the coal pits. We need to remember that cultivated people, including bishops, opposed any efforts to relieve these victims. Poverty, it was argued, taught the poor frugality. And this went on, though mitigated by the strenuous efforts of reformers, right through the nineteenth century. It still existed in the Edwardian era, and Charlie Chaplin's reminiscences have made that all too clear. Such things do return unless there be a vigilance to detect and oppose them.

It was a growing awareness of these things that led Morris to Socialism. E. P. Thompson's book shows how this man took steps into a harder life than probably he had ever contemplated. He took on what, judged from one angle, could only be progressively a story of failure. His biographer Professor Mackail said, 'Some people, even those who knew him well, thought of his Socialism as a sudden and unaccountable aberration.' He was not the first man or women to be called mad in choosing a way of life that challenged the way of the world.

Morris had not much use for the Christian Church as he saw it in contemporary society. Though his firm made windows for churches, the Christianity that Morris held to would have been questioned. My point is that he stepped out of his comfortable class world, and followed a way of life that was harsh, demanding, dispiriting, and draining of life for the sake of the poor of the Earth. I think he belongs to the communion of saints, because 'greater love can no man show ...' He took the decision and never went back on it. From 1880 to the end of 1896 he wore himself out with the hurly burly of it all, speaking all over the country at street ends and in clubs to win adherents to socialism. Even in 1880 he confessed: 'The whole thing seems too tangled to see through and too heavy to move.'

The situation was indeed complex. On the one hand there was a real stirring again of social thinking and purpose. Popular education, public libraries, cheaper books and public readings were all beginning to create new expectations. The most hard

hitting of Dicken's novels, *Hard Times*, had pilloried the rancid
individualism and the social muddle of class divisions. The most
outspoken of Ruskin's writings *Unto this last* had so shocked the
editor of Cornhill Magazine, Thackeray, that he refused to continue their publication. The 1880s saw a new wave of political
purpose that gave the trade unions more power, reawakening the
spirit which had given Chartism its fire. When the first great
TUC procession made its way into Hyde Park in 1890 it was
watched approvingly by an elderly white-bearded man who
remarked, 'The grandchildren of the Chartists are entering the
struggle.' He was Frederick Engels. In the Socialist League,
which Morris took part in after breaking with the SDF, he was
working with Eleanor Marx. Those were years of great turbu-
lence and violence. Bloody Sunday in Trafalgar Square in 1887,
the London Dock Strike, the continual troubles in the coalfields,
all made it evident that a new impetus had been given to
Socialist intention. But there was little political education. Morris
wrote in 1885, 'I want an educated movement. Discontent is not
enough, though it is natural and inevitable. The discontented
must know what they are aiming at.' It was in this area that confusion reigned. Was it to be by building up a new political party
to concentrate on Parliamentary action? Was it to be by using
the new Local Government institutions, mainly schools?

Morris's line was clear, 'My belief is that the old order can
only be overthrown by force; for that reason it is all the more
necessary that the revolution shall be not an ignorant but an
intelligent revolution.' One is bound to ask, 'What force? And
what intelligence?' The education that Morris rightly required
was not there. One must go on to ask about today, 'How is it to
be put there?' Who was then to teach the masses of working
men and women to see the true nature of society and their place
in it? The SDF, the ILP, the Fabians, the Anarchists were all
there, but they barely touched the great mass of people.

It seems that the churches had failed to take opportunities
here; because, by and large, they were not sensitive enough to
human needs, but were too concerned about their own thing.
There were some stirrings in the Church, certainly, and I quote
some instances that might raise eyebrows today.

At the Pan Anglican Congress (1887) a bishop read a paper on Socialism and Christianity, urging amongst other things the setting up of a University Chair in Christian Sociology.

At the Lambeth Conference in 1888, the Archbishop said that 'no more important problems could well occupy attention than such as are connected with what is popularly known as Socialism.'

In 1889 the President of the Christian Social Union, Bishop Westcott, spoke on Individualism and Socialism, stressing the theme that the Socialist regard for mankind as an organic whole to be brought to fullness of life was a fundamental tenet of the Christian faith.

In 1908 Bishop Gore declared to the Pan Anglican Congress that: 'We must identify ourselves with the great impeachment of our industrial system. We must refuse to acquiesce to it. But more than this, we must identify ourselves, because we are Christians, with the positive ethical ideal of Socialism.'

Finally, some words of a Regius Professor of Divinity in Oxford (Goudge): 'Two things may be said about the Christ and both are important. The first is that the Christ is always the bringer of a corporate, not an individual salvation ... the second is that the thought of Christ is in the closest connection with the thought of the Kingdom. He comes to overthrow all that hinders that Kingdom ... so that the discontent with and hatred of the unjust system is a thing which which Christians ought to sympathize.... If we persist in identifying ourselves with the system and its evils, woe to us all.'

Now Morris during those last years of his life slogged away at street meetings all over England, besides editing *The Commonweal* and many pamphlets. He died worn out in 1896. One is bound to say that while his contributions like those of the Church leaders I have quoted, and those of Charles Booth in his famous survey of Labour in London, of Rowntree in his study of poverty in York and C. P. Masterman in his book *The Condition of England* all helped towards the teaching of Socialism, yet they failed to produce a strong, educated, purposeful movement capable of laying the foundation for a new and different social order in Britain.

Here we are, a century later facing that problem still. We should have learned at least that the way forward is never simple or straight, but two steps forward and one backward, again and again, also that Morris and his kind are not to be set aside and forgotten because they were so obviously defeated. 'We must get used to defeats,' he wrote, 'and refuse to be discouraged by them. I'm an old hand at that game, my life having passed in being defeated.' But he knew well that we are only truly defeated if we fail to learn from the defeats.

So, keeping Morris in mind, let us pay him the honour of learning from him, rejoicing in the human fellowship he so truly extolled, and setting to work to hammer out the programme of education for Christian Socialism today. Let us assert plainly that the true foundations of political liberty, personal and social welfare are in the Gospel. The Gospel ceaselessly reminds us that all human beings form one single people. 'From one ancestor he made all nations to dwell on the face of the earth' (Acts of the Apostles 17.26).

In the implementation of that belief there are four features to be observed:

1 *Ethical.* A straightforward hatred of any system that stunts and corrupts human relationships by reducing people to being a means of profit; a seeking by contrast the forming of a community of responsible men and women, working together without fear in fellowship for common ends and full personal development.

2 *Political.* The development of institutions which serve the people equally, testing them for their contribution, not only to economic welfare but to welfare in the widest sense, of justice, human dignity, health, freedom of speech.

3 *Cultural.* To provide for the full access of all people to the enjoyment of the arts and sciences, so that they may be truly heirs of the whole inheritance of human experience.

4 *Practical.* Using as fully as possible the historical insights, and imaginative wealth of the arts and religious experience to illuminate the common good, always endeavouring to understand. 'Don't let it make you bitter; the world's bitter enough already. Try to understand' (James Baldwin).

One of the most valuable sayings of Morris, which seemed so vital to me that it was writ large in my parish church in Sheffield, is 'Fellowship is heaven: lack of fellowship is hell.' This may be an increasingly important way of surviving any disintegration of society. Alistair MacIntyre calls for the construction of new forms of community within which the moral life can be sustained. This will enable us to survive what he sees as the coming age of barbarism and darkness.

One great gain for the present, for achieving this task, is that women now have a fuller part in the Socialist Movement, and nurture is having a fuller share in fashioning the movement.

And through recent calamities and known hazards to the environment, a full gain comes within sight, that of understanding our right relationship with the created world: to perceive the glory in creation, that Morris and many poets rejoice in, and learn to use its resources without destroying them, for God's sake.

16

ON MARRIAGE

After the reading of St Paul's great eloquent testimony to love in
1 Corinthians 13, it might well seem frivolous to add anything
more. But St Paul was hardly enthusiastic about marriage –
which is our real concern now. So I want to take you back for a
moment to childhood experience, and then on to a couple of
lines by an English poet that will carry us further.

That moment was the day, I feel sure, when someone held a
shell to our ear, that we might listen, they said, to the soft surg-
ing of the sea: a moment of *wonder*, the wonder that you can see
in a child's eyes as he or she listens to it, the moment of wonder
that Shakespeare gave us in *The Tempest* when Ferdinand first saw
Miranda and exclaimed, 'Oh – you wonder'. It was just such a
moment that led a poet I have in mind to write a couple of lines
that are memorable, even if the rest of his poem is forgotten.

> Love still has something of the sea
> From whence his mother rose.

Now to try to speak about the sea, about love, and about marriage is too much for us unless we keep this sense of *wonder* in the
very forefront of our mind and senses.

There was therefore something of value in that old Jewish
practice of endeavouring to say in as few words as possible what
really mattered most in life and the great occasions and
moments of wonder in it, choosing them carefully like pearls to
be threaded together and handled with reverence.

So, when they said: 'Two that sit together, occupied with the
Torah, with the Law of God, have the Shekinah between them,'
that is, the Glory of God, his very Presence. And when one great
teacher, hearing the footsteps of his mother, stood up and said:
'I will arise before the Glory of God which approaches,' so they

also said, 'Between husband and wife dwells the Shekinah' – which is the utmost you can say about it – and the cue for our *sense of wonder*.

We come to it, as to any new dimension in life, having to learn its true ways exactly as we once had to learn to walk and to talk, and in adolescence to discover ourselves and selves other than our own.

We have to grow into it continually making new ventures together, because we only become what *we do*, not just dream or think aloud. Growing in this way is a demanding, bewildering, but exhilarating process, uneven in pace, often dismaying, sometimes deeply painful. In marriage it always involves another person, bound to see things at every step through eyes other than our own, and so it is doubly difficult as well as being doubly rewarding.

It is full of quite contradictory and ambiguous things that we have to learn to hold together. Life is not logical but dialectical – which is why it calls for as much listening as speaking.

Now to the bride and bridegroom. First then, about *expectations*. You do right to expect everything good from it, for anything less would be to belittle the Shekinah, to fail to observe the glory. 'Therefore even with every comment of thy soul *observe*,' said Hamlet, and the moments of this true vision will come, and in them you will be 'ringed with living light'.

Just as surely you will need to remember that the two of you are limited human beings who cannot always rise to the occasion, cannot always keep in step with one another, cannot always recover graciously or repent humbly, cannot always see what to the one or other of you seems perfectly obvious!

Hold fast then to your expectations, but be charitably ready to start afresh from where both of you are, again and again and again in all your life together.

Second, as regards living in the world: 'Heaven and earth in little space' is a true description of marriage because it includes all aspects of life: ecstasy and washing up, romance and tedious chores, bliss and anxiety. And it is right that you should at times be able to exclude all else, and simply be all in all to each other.

But not all the time. Just as surely you must live in the world and do something that contributes to it, because you couldn't possibly have the Shekinah just to yourselves: you would just shrivel up in it. Your marriage, for better or worse, is a contribution to the total life shared by all human beings, and you must inspire and sustain each other in making it a worthwhile contribution to the common good, and pay the price for this not grudgingly but with magnanimity.

> Think, when our one soul understands
> The great *word* that makes all things new,
> When Earth breaks up or heaven expands,
> How will the change strike me and you
> In the house not made with hands?
> Oh, I must feel your brain prompt mine
> Your heart anticipate my heart –
> You must be just before, in fire
> See, and make me see in your part
> New depths in the Divine.

Not only see it – but do it.

It can never be easy to do this, and people often grow cynical about it, but we all know in our heart of hearts that we all long for it to be true of this latest marriage, that it may renew our high hopes for Life itself.

And third: about the kind of attitude on which everything turns: 'A marriage equally rich in every season is an exception!'

If people realized and remembered this they might face the not-so-good times more cheerfully, and be more patient with each other and themselves. The pledge in marriage is not a reckless gamble but a sober, brave declaration of intent, of will and purpose, to be renewed over and over again as long as you both shall live. In the strength of that purpose you can tackle all things, and find from your own experience that it needs no other justification.

So the things that belong to the Shekinah – the glory, beauty, generosity, patience, gentleness and loving kindness will be yours and continue to be yours, if you go on committing yourselves to this concern for a loving relationship between yourselves and the wider world.

The unpractised eye and heart cannot help making mistakes, but mistakes, faults, even sins, matter much less than the direction in which you look, the perception you have of what it means. Marriage is not a Botticellian cockleshell, nor a cruise in a luxury liner, but as one poet put it,

> Bound fast in love
> Sharing the storm-tossed raft that was
> And is our life, defying wintry weather
> And wind-whipped waves that slap our creaking planks
> O'er saving hope and find prayer
> To cling together
> Still loving, fiercely one, until the last.

You are heirs together of the grace of Life, you can come into your inheritance and it is wonderfully rich: it enriches Life itself. Amen!

17

THE TRANSFIGURATION

St John's real moment of transfiguration was when he saw Jesus on his knees washing the disciples' feet. John grasped the vision, but we are afraid. Our temptation is to institutionalize, sacramentalize, theologize, anything that takes it out of the day-to-day living of work, marriage, friendship, and contact with the earth. Such abstraction leads to hierarchy, which gives little hope for transfiguration. Just occasionally, however, someone bursts through like St Francis or William Blake. Indeed, to some extent every artist gets the same perception. Traherne, I think, has this the most: 'What a wondrous thing that in my body lies.'

Transfiguration is a momentary thing, but it is enough to have seen it. Most of the time we go around with glazed eyes. Yet we do get glimpses occasionally, particularly in people. I have in fact only seen one person transfigured. It was at the birth of her first child when a young mother in my parish looked absolutely radiant in every respect. After a while the radiance left her.

In the Church there is little scope for transformation, but I remember seeing one strange woman who had been brought up in a workhouse and had been fetched out of it by an uncle for whom she kept house. One day she wandered into church, heard an invitation to a meeting. She came to it and she was transformed. She came to church each week and inspired even the laconic. She took Christ at his word. Indeed, she had a degree of personal humility that would leave most of us standing.

When house-to-house visiting I met a former forgeman whose great passion in life was birds. He would get up at 4 a.m. before his 6 a.m. shift to watch birds on the outskirts of Sheffield. He had a tobacco box in which he put odd feathers which he would turn over as though they were pure gold. One day he saw a hawk. It was to him an absolute glimpse of glory.

THE ALAN ECCLESTONE LIBRARY

published by Cairns Publications

Gather the Fragments
A Book of Days
compiled by Alan Ecclestone
and edited by Jim Cotter
1993

Alan Ecclestone
Priest as Revolutionary
A Biography by Tim Gorringe
1994

Through the Year
with Alan Ecclestone
1997

Firing the Clay
Occasional writings of Alan Ecclestone
1999